THE
MIDDLE
MIND

For John, Nick, Charlie, and David, whose respective geniuses have made the ongoing Normal years something extraordinary for me.

Contents

THE
MIDDLE
MIND

INTRODUCTION

Whoever can give his people better stories than the ones they live in is like the priest in whose hands common bread and wine become capable of feeding the very soul.

Hugh Kenner, *The Pound Era*

1.

One afternoon, about fifteen years ago, the artist Nicolas Africano and I were visiting a common friend, Bill Morgan, who was recovering from surgery in a hospital here in Normal, Illinois. We sat there talking, in an awkward nowhere, unsure of whether or not the simple facts of the situation were available for conversation. All I wanted was for the moment to be familiar. I wanted to be able to gossip and indulge in my habitually heightened sense of irony. But a different sort of reality was asserting itself: pain, uncertainty, physical disfigurement, maybe even good old Mr. Death. So, the scene was made by the discomfort of friends who had no access to their ordinary rapport and who were afraid to talk about what was right in front of them. Or at least that's how I felt. My options were crusty with, as Wallace Stevens might have put it, the quotidian, what you're "supposed to do." Our friend Bill was, of course, off in some sweet land of morphine indifference. But Nicolas, to my amazement, was somewhere I could never have anticipated. Apropos of nothing, he said, pointing to a length of clear plastic tubing suspended above us, "That amber light is beautiful." And there in fact was a tiny amber light in the middle of the tubing, a little light I hadn't noticed at all. It was bright like an isolated star. It triangulated us. Suddenly, the situation changed for me into something completely other than it had been the moment before. We'd been translated. Reordered. Nicolas's comment reconstellated us. I had a powerful feeling that everything had just been changed utterly and made—what other word was there for it?—*beautiful*. I smiled, suddenly happy. I looked at Nicolas in awe. And I thought: "You can do that?!"

The tiny amber light perched angelically above us functioned like Wallace Stevens's jar on a hill in Tennessee:

I placed a jar in Tennessee,
And round it was, upon a hill.
It made the slovenly wilderness
Surround that hill.

The other Tennessee, the real Tennessee, is annihilated by Stevens's jar, just as the quotidian world of hospitals and sick friends was destroyed by Nicolas's observation. His gesture—seizing on that which otherwise passes notice—is a metaphor for the world-making capacities of the imagination. My experience, I think, says something about the fact that the imagination is not only about creation; it is also about how we see and how we experience. We cannot create in a fresh and lively way while looking at our world from a stale (even if familiar and comforting) perspective. So, before the productive work of the imagination can begin, we must be outside of the familiar. Africano's subtle gesture "defamiliarized" in a moment. In an instant. Pop! He created a gap in which the imagination could do its work. The scene deployed itself differently, offering itself openly to the imagination. If I felt a little like laughing in that moment, it was because I intuited the opportunity and wondered what Bill—or his doctor!—would make of this "opportunity."

Of course, the quotidian version of things in which I had been slumbering was also an act of the imagination, just as Knoxville, Tennessee, is an act of the imagination to which we dedicate ourselves daily out of a mix of necessity, joy, fear, and habit. But mine was an act of the imagination that I would describe as crusted over, just as Knoxville is a city crusted over, and whatever town you're sitting in right now, be it large or small, is crusted over and much in need of someone like Africano to point over your head, just outside of your peripheral vision, where there is a little amber light that you've never noticed that wants very much to show you something you could not suspect without it.

Wallace Stevens's little book of essays, *The Necessary Angel* (1942), deserves far more relevance than it seems to have in the present. Stevens's book is intelligent, humane, and inventive in a way that we should want to value in the present and every other future present moment. The subtitle of this slim book is "Essays on Reality and the Imagination." What is extraordinary in Stevens's perception is his certainty that reality and the imagination do not stand different from and opposed to each other. They are in fact the same thing. Imagination "has the strength of reality or none at all." (7) The reality that we refer to as our daily reality is simply the work of the human imagination that has become ossified, codified, and generally naturalized. It is imagination that has achieved such consensus that it is an "of course." This is so in both a good and a bad sense. We need a shared reality because we need to live together, we need to be able to communicate, and we need to be able to trust that we're part of a shared world. This is ideology, or a shared imaginative understanding of the world, in its weak (meaning "neutral") and most inescapable sense. The authority to manage this shared understanding is what politics is about at its most basic level. Who will have the authority to say what kind of human world we will all live in? Who will have the authority to answer Wallace Stevens's question about "how to live, what to do"? This is ideology in its strong and most threatening sense. This ideology is about insisting on one human world as the true and only proper human world, and the first gesture of this ideology is always, of course, to say, "I'm not ideology. The world is a collection of static objects and behaviors arranged in space. Nature is stable and unchanging. The imagination is fantasy and if it has a place in our world it is a place like Fantasyland, carefully circumscribed by the walls of Disneyland. I won't utterly deny it, though I don't like it much, but I will limit its province." Limit and carefully monitor.

We're not much in the habit of poking at these dominant realities that are so much the "of course" of our lives. We're delicate. We're used to deferring. What parents, teachers, presidents, and media spokespeople like Dan Rather (the bosses in our social factory) say is good enough for us. We demur out of habit and fright over what *not* demurring might require of us. We sacrifice our lives out of a feeling that there is some sort of comfort in deferring. Do I dare to eat a peach, indeed.

For Stevens, the problem was one of equilibrium. "The relation between the imagination and reality is a question, more or less, of precise equilibrium." (9) That this relation was at the time he wrote a "failure" was not, for Stevens, a question. The only question was to ask why and to what degree it was a failure. The failure was due to "the pressure of reality." (13) As Stevens wrote, "By the pressure of reality, I mean the pressure of an external event or events on the consciousness to the exclusion of any power of contemplation." (20)

On the other side, for Stevens, the figure of the poet, standing in confrontation with reality, achieves near revolutionary stature. Even though he was an insurance executive, Stevens had a vision of the real that was politically radical. He argued, in words that describe our present moment to a frightening degree:

> In speaking of the pressure of reality, I am thinking of life in a state of violence, not physically violent, as yet, for us in America, but physically violent for millions of our friends and for still more millions of our enemies and spiritually violent, it may be said, for everyone alive. . . . A possible poet must be a poet capable of resisting or evading the pressure of the reality of this last degree, with the knowledge that the degree of today may become a deadlier degree tomorrow. (27)

But how emasculated and domesticated Stevens has become in the American literary canon. He is remembered for cute, metaphysical poems such as "The Emperor of Ice Cream." Practically something for children. This Stevens may cause us to smack our "muzzy bellies" in delight, but he won't cause us to change our lives. He is safely domesticated, made a friend to the quotidian, someone you read at the school-factory in the museum of the safely established canon. He is read now, if he is read at all, as an example of literary greatness, another culture hero, quite irrelevant to what happens when we get in our cars, go to work or the mall, turn on our TVs or computers. And this when what he wanted to say to us was, "You're being murdered"!

2.

As Stevens liked to put it, our imagination is in "poverty." What does this poverty mean in practical terms? Well, it's something we experience daily. Take our entertainment. Even when it's clever (which I acknowledge that it is at times, in the full superficiality that term implies), does it help us to understand that the present world is not the only God-given, natural, and inevitable world and that it could be different? Or does it stabilize the inevitability and naturalness of the present disposition of things? On the whole, our entertainment—movies, TV, music—is a testament to our ability and willingness to endure boredom . . . and pay for it. Our academics certainly provide us with something different from what entertainment provides, although that something is not necessarily less boring. But too often members of the postmodern professoriate (and I am speaking mainly to the humanities here) sound as if they live in some very distant world. Not an elite ivory tower as in the past, but something more like a strange, perhaps perverse, cult. A sort of Dungeons and Dragons with Ph.D.s.[1] And I would hope that I need to say nearly nothing about the apparatchiks that we call our elected representatives, they who do the bidding of

---

[1] I may have the wrong metaphor here. Thought and creativity have been "institutionalized" in our academies. I'm not sure if it's a prison or a madhouse or both. In any event, the inmates show little desire to "bust the joint."

their corporate owners. When was the last time you heard a politician make a public utterance to which you didn't want to reply, "Will you please shut up or say what you really think—assuming, God help us, you can think at all"?

Beyond these three broad categories of entertainment, academic orthodoxy, and political ideology (the three great enemies of the imagination with which I will have most to do in these pages), there is a vast world of the automatic in which we are sunk to our neck like some poor sinner in one of Dante's murkier *bolgias* in *The Inferno*. For instance, here in Central Illinois, it makes sense to people to think, "It's a good idea to plant corn to make into ethanol to put into our cars so that we can continue to undermine the present and future quality of our lives through [count the marvelous ways!] congestion, pollution, endless asphalting, stripping the nutrients from our topsoil, eroding the topsoil, traffic injuries and fatalities, and the spiritual damage of endless consumption, debt, and work." Of course, that's not exactly how it's put in these parts, to the degree that anyone at all feels obliged to articulate the social good of growing corn to put in our cars. I'm helping my friends and neighbors make a confession. I'm helping them bust out of the automatic. I'm frankly hard-pressed to say whether this instance— growing corn to put into cars—is an example of the poverty of the imagination or simply evidence that as a species we're too stupid to live.

There's no need to stop there. What evidence of imaginative wealth does the sea-to-shining-sea strip-malling of America provide? When exactly did we all decide that every Main Street in these United States should look exactly the same, with exactly the same corporate eateries—Applebee's unto Bennigan's unto Olive Garden—punctuated by Wal-Marts and Best Buys all sitting on the shoreline of an inexhaustible automobile busyness? When did we as a nation sit down and say, "That's how I'd like to live, by gar"? And what evidence of imaginative wealth do our vinyl-clad, prefab suburbs—the real national nightmare on Elm Street—present? These places make Malvina Reynolds's "little boxes made of ticky-tacky" (still perched on the hillside in Daly City, California) look like a utopian moment that we somehow overlooked and now must long for plangently.

So, my intention in this book is to explore this poverty, *our* poverty, through the media, academia, and politics, the three areas of public life that provide the vehicles for the great antagonists of the imagination: entertainment, orthodoxy, and ideology. But I also want to think, more positively, about the present condition of our religious and civic spirit, as well as about something that I will call the sublime, that which beckons to us beyond the suffocating if familiar activities of entertainment, academic orthodoxy, and ideology. The sublime is that indistinct but essential thing that Stevens called the "necessary angel." It has something very simple if curiously distant to say to us. It wants to tell us that change is real and the world can be other than it is. Think of the next four sections of this introduction as overtures to these efforts.

Back in his glory days with Talking Heads, David Byrne wrote a song called "Found a Job." The scene he described concerned a family that is bored with TV and decides it will make its own TV shows.

> *Judy's in the bedroom, inventing situations.*
> *Bob is on the street today, scouting up locations.*
> *They've enlisted all their family.*
> *They've enlisted all their friends.*

The song concludes, "If your work isn't what you love, then something isn't right."

Byrne describes a tension that is fundamental and inescapable between capitalism and the populations it organizes. Our culture provides entertainment as a compensation for and an inducement to work. It reconciles work and leisure, and reconciles production and consumption. It eliminates contradictions that would otherwise be intolerable. "This is what I get for my lost years in the corporate carrel? Fox programming? Reality TV? Hot babes in halter-tops eating insects? COPS? I might as well get a billy club and beat myself up. I think I'd feel better about it all." When we recognize that the "entertainment" is boring and dishonest, and the daily work is unfulfilling, resentment begins to grow. What we feel is disdain for what has been provided for us, especially in light of what we might produce if our own creativity were free. In contrast with the needs of capitalism, creativity (the work of the imagination) is a messy plurality of human possibilities not conducive to economic efficiency. And so capitalism has always had to find ways to orient this messy plurality to the business at hand: work. As capitalism's great friend Walt Disney put it, "It's off to work we go." Happily. Whistling. Full of a sense of virtue. With pickaxes, no less. In the twentieth and twenty-first centuries, this control has had less to do with the raw, repressive, physical obligation to work (although that is not absent, and is certainly not absent in Asian sweatshops and the *maquiladoras* of Mexico) and more to do with managing our creativity. We American workers are more beguiled than we are oppressed.

In the present, capitalism cannot entirely deny creativity without risking another sixties-style flight from business-as-usual. Capitalism will always be vulnerable to the fact that people can refuse its world, as many did under Timothy Leary's call to "drop out." On the one hand, Leary seemed a silly, druggy fraud and no real threat to anyone. But he said something terrifyingly simple and direct that was echoed throughout the culture: you don't have to live this way; do something else. At that time, Leary was simply the most recent incarnation of the spirit of refusal. Paul Goodman's *Growing Up Absurd* and Herbert Marcuse's *One-dimensional Man* preceded him. This spirit of refusal was and is driven by the question, as Goodman put it, of what it means "to grow up into such a fact as: 'During my productive years I will spend eight hours a day doing what is no good.'" (29)

Since the Reagan Revolution, Leary's call has not been broadly taken up, although the occasional indie/alternative rock band like Talking Heads, films like Richard Linklater's *Slacker,*[2] and the punk

---

[2] One might add the cartoon strip *Dilbert* to this list. *Dilbert* certainly expresses the idea that work is "absurd" and "not good." But in my hometown newspaper, *Dilbert* appears in the *business* section. There is no edge of refusal in *Dilbert,* however stupid, boring, wasteful, and dehumanizing it may think the corporate world to be. It asks people in their corporate carrels to laugh at their situation . . . and get back to work.

and slacker subcultures have kept the idea of refusal of capitalism's world alive. But my point is that the tension between the imperative to work and the human need to be free to create one's own world is fundamental and inescapable. The imagination is real, and its defining concept is freedom. Without freedom it cannot do its work and so cannot be itself. No amount of End of History, End of Irony, New World Order, we-beat-the-Commies self-congratulation will alter this fact. There will always be people (especially young people) who will understand that "getting a job" is an assault on what their intuition tells them it means to be alive. They'll always just a little or maybe a lot resent it, that job. And that resentment will always be a threat to capitalism's order. Not for nothing were the following words attached to the entrance of the Sorbonne in May 1968:

> We are inventing a new and original world. Imagination is seizing power. (quoted in Roszak, 22)

That being the case, what capitalism can do is *manage* our creativity. Its primary strategy is to provide the work of the imagination for us. This is a strategy that Herbert Marcuse called "repressive freedom." For instance, Walt Disney has for decades represented the American imagination both to the world and to Americans themselves. More recently, Steven Spielberg's DreamWorks has made it possible for Spielberg and members of his company (working under very clear limitations) to be creative so that the rest of us can continue working. But even Spielberg and company are mere "content providers" for something that is in the last reckoning not art but commodity.

The programming in movies, television, computers, and our stereos simulates the human imagination; it functions as an imagination prosthetic. Insofar as your high-end audio equipment means you won't produce any music yourself, won't even listen to live music, won't know what it feels like to capture the rhythms and textures of music in your own hands and lungs, how playing music changes your relationship to music and changes music's relationship to the world, your stereo system is a musical wooden leg. It is literally a dis-ability.[3] Worse yet, this dis-ability leaves substantial control over the "content" of these systems in the hands of giant international entertainment corporations like Sony and BMG.

The value of such prosthetics to business-as-usual is threefold: they neutralize a possible complaint from subjects ("Your life isn't creative?! What about *Shreck?* What about those little cute Muppets? Kermit the Frog? That's not creative?"); they allow for efficiency because the work is done by a few people (trusted to paint by the ideological numbers) rather than by the population as a whole (Judy and Bob are at work, not "scouting up locations"); and they actually become part of the economic system by making products, profits, *and* ideological justifications of the system as a whole. So successful has this "imagination" industry been in the last half-century that it is now among the largest and most profitable export commodities for the United States. (In the next chapter, I'll look at this conjunction of product, profit, and ideology in detail through a reading of Spielberg's *Saving Private Ryan.*)

In short, forget the Emersonian tradition of Self-Reliance. We're not even Do-It-Yourself Hobbyists. We're a Done-Elsewhere-by-Somebody-Else Culture.

Even "high" culture requires duplicity of this kind. The dominant order arranges for the appearance of a "serious" culture, apart from the entertainment biz, but what it provides is usually not all that different from the entertainment industry in the end. The great vehicle for this duplicity is what I call the Middle Mind. The culture informed by the strategies of the Middle Mind promises intelligence, seriousness, care, but what it provides in reality is something other. What the Middle Mind does best is flatten distinctions. It turns culture into mush. One

---

[3]*Stereophile* magazine regularly runs interviews with musicians and is regularly dismayed at what crummy audio rigs they have. The indifference of musicians to the high-tech world of the audiophile is the source of considerable wonderment and pain to the editors of *Stereophile.*

of the great exemplars of the Middle Mind is Terry Gross's NPR program *Fresh Air*. *Fresh Air* presents cultural programming through interviews with classical musicians (Christoph Eschenbach) and banal pop musicians (Barry Manilow); genuine novelistic innovators (David Foster Wallace) and hack realists; cinema geniuses (Jim Jarmusch) and TV drudges (Judd Apatow of *Undeclared*). *Fresh Air* never acknowledges any incongruity in its choice of guests. *It's all good*, as they say. And it's all useless for the purposes of intelligence. It is, in the final account, just more "content." Something to sell. It's a threat to no one nowhere. Which isn't to say that we should expect Terry Gross to be a spokesperson for revolution. What we should expect is that a program on culture shouldn't stifle the imagination. *Fresh Air* offers to us no defamiliarizing amber lights, no jars on a hill. *Fresh Air* is a purveyor. It purveys entertainment as art and thought.

When my essay "The Middle Mind" appeared in *Context* and the "Readings" section of *Harper's* (March 2002), the criticism, as revealed in letters to the editor, was predictable. People felt personally insulted. Because they listened to Terry Gross or considered themselves "fans," it was as if I were telling them they were members of a class of fools. (I have, I think, with great tact refrained from that judgment.) It was as if the question I was asking were something out of the *Parade* Sunday supplement. "Are You Middle-Minded? Answer these ten easy questions and find out!" And, of course, if I was telling them that they were inferior for listening to *Fresh Air*, that made me "snooty," an "elitist," and a "snob." Let me say this directly: the high/low culture distinction is not what I'm interested in and does not provide a useful or revealing register for talking about contemporary culture. It is one of the principal purposes of this book to argue how and why that's so. The Middle Mind is a *strategy*. It is a means to an end. It is a form of *management*.

Although Terry Gross's two million fans may never get beyond their sense of personal hurt to acknowledge it, *Fresh Air* is not somehow uniquely the problem. *Charlie Rose* is equally culpable. Few things in cultural programming in the mass media are quite as disturbing as watching Charlie Rose leaning forward, craning out over his table, peering deeply, on the very precipice of an incisive question sure to reveal a real Idea, a slim, almost excited smile starting to form on his lips as he imagines the dawning joy of the intellectual life revealed for himself and his audience, and we move with the camera, oh-so-sincerely, to his guest and see that all this expectation and anticipation is addressed to . . . Lance Armstrong. Or Ron "Opie" Howard. Or Gary Shandling (who at least had the decency to look uncomfortably bemused on the other end of such fraudulent expectations [but then looking uncomfortably bemused is Shandling's stock in trade]). No matter, all that Rose's efforts yielded from his side was a *pedo puro* of inquiry anyway. Even if he'd had Leonardo (da Vinci, not Di Caprio) on the other end, there would have been nothing for him to discover given his deadening approach to the life of the mind. So, in the end, Lance Armstrong and Ron Howard work out fine. We have the lovely pretense of serious inquiry, no one gets hurt, and no one has to worry that something undesirable might come of it.

Like a demand for real thought. We are free to say anything we like as long as what we say does not suggest, to paraphrase Noam Chomsky, that the ruling order has no right to rule. Says Mr. John Q. Public of Anytown, USA, "Corporate culture is good for business and business is good for me. Why, without business I wouldn't have a job. The culture it provides is entertaining. Some of the culture it provides is even good to eat. I like it fine, and my kids love it to death. It's *fun*. So what's the problem?"

The problem for earlier theorists like Dwight Macdonald, in his classic essay "A Theory of Mass Culture," was that the market-driven culture of petit bourgeois *kitsch* was destroying both folk culture and high culture. Macdonald was right to see that the mass culture he examined was finally about managing political consent. This is also the Middle Mind's function. But other aspects of his theory turned out not to be quite so prescient. Contemporary cultural critics are right to complain of Macdonald's nostalgia for highbrow avant-gardism and "authentic" folk art. Macdonald predicted a "dark" future for high culture because he felt that mass culture would tend persistently to "water it down." In fact, I think it's more accurate to say that since the sixties and the arrival of postmodern hybridization of high and low cultures, just the opposite has happened: high culture has made popular culture richer. Mass culture has gotten smarter and more technically adroit when there has been sufficient genius to take advantage of the opportunity, which is to say that popular art has gotten richer on its progressive margins. A pop musician like Beck is a working encyclopedia of styles. When pop musicians like Beck are interviewed, they're likely to have Mingus or Messiaen on in the background. There clearly is visual, linguistic, and technical brilliance in a culture that has produced David Lynch's *Eraserhead*, Philip Glass's *The Photographer*, Laurie Anderson's musical/narrative/visual artwork *USA*, Mark Leyner's avant-pop *Et Tu, Babe*, Coppola's *Apocalypse Now*, Elvis Costello and the Brodsky String Quartet's *The Juliet Letters*, Nina Hagen's outrageous and charming synthesis of punk and operatic coloratura, Keith Haring, Kenny Scharf's pop-surrealism, Frank Zappa's "strictly genteel" and perfectly brilliant blending of doo-wop, rock guitar improvisation, and Varese-inspired orchestral music in *Burnt Weeny Sandwich*; and this doesn't begin to touch on what's happened in jazz with John Coltrane, Charles Mingus, Ornette Coleman, and many others, or, for literature, in postmodernism's playful appropriation of sci-fi and detective genre fiction. The interest and sophistication of the most progressive elements on the margins of mass culture cannot be in question. This is not a dark story of devolution requiring nostalgia for the old days of highbrow quality or folk art authenticity. It is about the capacity within art for social antagonism, and it is finally about strategies for managing that antagonism. Hence, the Middle Mind.

3.

I hope it's clear by this point that the "imagination" I am interested in is not the romantic imagination of genius. It is not a metaphysical or idealist quality. It is not a little walnut-shaped thing in your brain. It is nothing in itself. I am not talking about the imagination because I think it would be nice if we could be creative in the way that the mother of a third grader might wish that there were more art instruction at the local elementary school (although I'm not opposed to that). I am interested in the imagination as a social force that allows for both critique and reinvention. This is something that happens not only in art (although it happens most powerfully in art), but in every area of the culture—even in technology and science.

Having said that, it might seem surprising that from my perspective the academy (especially the humanities, especially especially English departments) is another enemy of the imagination. The American university is not itself a part of the Middle Mind, whose realm is strictly speaking the world of entertainment, but it is a mostly unwitting ally to the Middle Mind, a sort of "conceptual co-conspirator" as national security agents like to say, and their respective "spheres of influence" overlap in revealing ways. The contemporary university shares with the entertainment industry its simple institutional inertia, which tends to "manage" through sheer gravitational force. Professional norms and so-called dominant "critical paradigms" tend to stabilize in much the same way that assumptions about "consumer demand" make television programming predictable. ("People want sit-coms. They like COPS. We're only giving them what they want.")

The university also shares with the Middle Mind the tendency to flatten distinctions. This is most conspicuous in what has become known as "Cultural Studies," where, notoriously, Milton has had to share the stage with Madonna for the last two decades. In monolithic institutional environments, whether the media or the academy, where distinctions make no difference, it is very difficult for the imagination to do what it must do: create an outside, create distance, create possibility. In the context of the Middle Mind and the contemporary university, all our freedoms to think and to create are repressive in spite of themselves, creative-writing seminars notwithstanding. We become mere participants in or, worse yet, mere functions of the entertainment or educational systems in which we try to live.

And yet it seems very odd to me that the contemporary humanities, which began with deconstruction's distrust of truth-claims, moved very quickly to certainty, conviction, and even self-righteousness during the ascendancy of Cultural Studies.[4] This self-certainty (often referred to by conservatives as "political correctness") has had a stifling effect on the role of art as a material practice, as something involved with history and technique. Sadly, it means very little in the present to say, as T. S. Eliot said of Ezra Pound, that Pound was a better poet because he was *"il miglior fabbro,"* the better maker.

One of Cultural Studies' primary and facile convictions is that we are not who we are because of some original essence; we are who we are because of "social construction." We are determined by our social matrix. We are made subjects to a dominant social organization. We have "subject positions," not humanity, in a vast "apparatus." The rhetoric of this brand of Cultural Studies, with its constant appeal to "discursive formations" and "subject positions," has created a great, abstract, rationalist scholasticism within the humanities. I will have more to say about what's wrong with this thinking in Chapter Two, but let me first indulge the determinist fantasy of "social construction" and confess my own determinants, because I think it will shed some light on my arguments and on the academy as a whole.

I began studying literature, criticism, philosophy, and writing in 1969 at the University of San Francisco. At that time, New Criticism was still the unchallenged state of the art for reading, for criticism, and for constructing arguments about the importance of the study of literature, art, and ideas. New Criticism rejected extra-literary considerations for reading literature. For New Critics, a poem was an organic creation and each poem had to be approached on its own terms. One of New Criticism's leading proponents, Cleanth Brooks, formalized its

---

[4] To be perfectly accurate, I'd have to say that the present critical dominant is a hybrid of Cultural Studies and New Historicism, but with that caveat in mind and fearing that my reader might drift off into a coma-like state if I persisted in such fine distinctions, I find it sufficient for present purposes to refer to the mongrel mess as Cultural Studies.

methodology as "close reading." The assumption of close reading was that the text was finally whole or organic, but that it was also complex and often contained a paradox or an irony that needed to be explicated in order to understand fully the work's coherence and meaning. The job of the critic, and thousands of English majors from sea to shining sea, was to identify the paradox, resolve it, and thus reveal the work's full and profound import. When I started college in 1969, the assumptions of close reading had achieved something like the state of nature for me, my young peers, and my professors alike. Little could we suspect that just when New Criticism seemed most codified and stable, it was in fact most frail and about to crumble.

Just a few years later, in 1973, when I went to study writing at the Johns Hopkins University, I began to hear strange and hardly credible rumors from down a very implausible corridor at the end of which was the just-a-little-bit-scandalous office of Richard Macksey. Macksey was the iconoclastic professor who brought Jacques Derrida, Jacques Lacan, Roland Barthes, Michel Foucault, and others to the United States in 1966 for a conference at Hopkins that produced the seminal anthology *The Languages of Criticism and the Sciences of Man*. Poststructuralism was dawning and, oh my, things were changing.

By 1975, I was at the University of Iowa, thrown into a graduate seminar taught by Derrida scholar Gayatri Spivak in which the primary subject before us was deconstruction. Although Derrida had not created the idea of deconstruction as a means of challenging New Criticism, it wasn't long until Derrida's American readers, most of whom were in English departments, began to see the philosophical implications of deconstruction for New Critical procedures. New Criticism in its search for the "truth of the text" was a mere "purveyor of truth," in Derrida's telling phrase. New Criticism in all its institutional might was quickly devastated by deconstruction's critique of its pretensions to know the truth of the text. American New Critics had nothing like the philosophic sophistication they would need to combat this French attack on our reading practices. Clearly, everything I thought I knew about the work of the literary scholar or critic was now in doubt, and the future was up for grabs—especially *my* future, because it was a real race for me to come to terms with Derrida before I was given the institutional heave-ho. That old anxiety aside, the feeling that things are up for grabs has always been a feeling I've liked.

At the same time that I was studying with Spivak, however, I was also studying poetry with Merle Brown. Brown was a student of F. R. Leavis,[5] and one of the last standard-bearers of reading in the New Critical tradition. That is, he was still trying to move "close reading" forward by making new discoveries about what poems *do* and why that should matter to us as human beings. He was interested in the poem as a performance or an act. I met with Brown weekly in my first year at Iowa to discuss poems by Wallace Stevens. What I recall most clearly is how angry he would become when my comments on a poem failed the poem (this was not a rare thing and usually required the use of the word "glib" three or four times). I also recall how his reading could reveal the poem, make it bang forth, not as a meaning or interpretation but as a human and artistic performance of great power and suggestiveness. What I learned was that to have this sort of relationship with a poem, you had to live with it for days. Me and the poem, in the library, waiting for it to come to life, or waiting for my brain to come to the life of the poem that was always there patiently waiting for me.

Of course, Brown and Spivak despised each other. Both scholars sat on my comprehensive exam committee, and I think Merle felt betrayed by the fact that my approach to the committee's questions was informed more by deconstruction and Spivak than it was by New Criticism and Brown. Brown could not allow himself to open to the beauties of Derrida's way of doing philosophy, but I think he intuited something about the future that I could not: "Curtis, whatever deconstruction's virtues may be in themselves, it means nothing good, here on our shores, for the reading or writing of poetry." Although I think

---

[5]Oddly, the origin of British Cultural Studies is often credited to another of Leavis's students, Raymond Williams, who created what was known as Left Leavisism.

Brown was right in the long run, I blame Derrida for all this about as much as I blame Marx for Stalin's determination to make Shosta-kovich write theme songs for the Revolution.

4.

Bad as things surely are within the worlds of the Middle Mind and the academy, they're only worse and more frightening in the world of the social imagination as it is presided over by the narratives of politicians and their allies in business, the professions, and the military—what so-ciologist C. Wright Mills called the "power elite." But for whom and for what does this "elite," led by its C-student president, tell its tales?

After all, the traditional nation-state and its companion dream of a common culture (Deutschland, Old England) are being fast-tracked by a host of acronyms (NAFTA, IMF, WTO, EEU) onto the ash heap of history. Gone with them is any reason for patriotism. And yet the narratives of country and love of country are more ubiquitous now than at any time since Pearl Harbor, as we have been told repeatedly. These narratives of terrorism, of good triumphing over evil, are men-dacities. Of course, the truth isn't much prettier. The truth is that busi-ness internationalizes itself with the blessing of the state because in the final analysis its needs are more important than the needs of the people in its country of origin, the same people who are asked to swal-low (and who in fact *do* swallow) the fairy tales of even lousy story-tellers like George W. Bush. Is General Motors a company of the United States of America? Ask the people of Flint, Michigan, as Michael Moore did, famously, in *Roger and Me*. General Motors is of and for the Country of Exchange Value, a.k.a. money. And that, fi-nally, is the country to which Bush and the "power elite" are faithful.

If living together obliges human communities to imagine the meaning of their living together, what their culture means, then rather than living by "old men's lies" (Pound), let us live as Wallace Stevens's "freed men," freed exactly from fatal doctrine.

Tired of the old descriptions of the world,
The latest freed man rose at six and sat
On the edge of his bed. He said,
"I suppose there is
A doctrine to this landscape. Yet, having just
Escaped from the truth, the morning is color and mist,
Which is enough. . . ."

We are no closer to this freedom than we were in 1917, when Pound described us rising to "factitious bait." This is the broadest and most conspicuous poverty, a poverty of the social imagination, and it is before us daily in the headlines in our newspapers. It is only surprising that we can still manage to choke down our coffee and donuts over those "old lies . . . age old and age thick." (Pound)

It is not the case that there are no compelling accounts of our present situation. There are. But they are nearly universally sequestered, just as our creativity is sequestered, either by what amounts to a sort of media blacklisting of people like Noam Chomsky and Howard Zinn, or by presenting the work as "academic," a product of universities for academics only. There are certainly powerful exceptions, and it is very hopeful to see that the honest and combative work of writers like Andrei Codrescu, Bill Moyers, Molly Ivins, Tom Frank, Michael Moore, George W. S. Trow, Michael Bérubé, Mark Crispin Miller, and Eric Schlosser transcends the extended joke of two-party politics and urges people to reconsider the meaning of their world. These are smart, serious people who, unlike advocates of Cultural Studies, actually manage to broadly engage people and ideas. It is a profoundly good thing that some of their work is among "best-sellers" (in spite of the obvious self-defeating danger which that "product" designation holds in the world of the Middle Mind). What these writers instruct us in is the need for a cultural criticism that is smart, that thinks against the grain of dominant narratives, and that doesn't permit itself to be isolated in the self-interested professionalism or obscure and self-defeating jargons of the academy. Without such work we will be left with impoverished and impoverishing versions of our world among which the Bush family sagas about Saddam and Evil Empires will seem as credible as any other narrative available to us. We need to be able to think our world in ways that are perhaps iconoclastic but also potentially revealing. In the present case, in Chapter Three, "The Great American Disaster Machine," I will attempt to illuminate our national political imagination by revealing it as dependent upon what I call the technological imagination.

In spite of 9-11, the ongoing war against terror, the bankruptcy of some of the largest corporations in the United States, and the precipitous crash of the stock market in 2001–2, it is generally business as usual for the social imagination in our culture. Of course, it is entirely within the power of the "multitude" (the people, the public, us, what you will) to unsay the stability of that social imaginary. Why and how we ought to consider the unsaying of dominant narratives is the problem and the subject before us.

5.

I suppose that it is customary with books of this kind to pause after all the depressing criticism of the world-as-it-stands in order to offer a few suggestions of a more positive kind meant to give readers a little guidance and hope. I am willing to do so, and in fact I *do* so in Chapter Four, "The Highway of Despair Leads to a World in Love," and Chapter Five, "Notes Toward the Next American Sublime." But I offer my remedies, if you can call them that, with bemusement. I think you will see that my prescriptions for a return to a healthy social imagination are pretty plainly out of keeping with the temper of the time. Not surprisingly, given what I've said to this point, I will argue that we need to allow the imagination and its impulses to instability and change a central role (an incorrigible part of me wants to say a "promiscuous" role) in our national conversation about our shared future. Let art out of the museum and out of the university. Deinstitutionalize it. Take off the straitjacket of philanthropic support. Defeat the corporate ownership of what little imagination we have.

The Telecommunications Act of 1996, substantially written by industry lobbyists, deregulated radio and telephone markets, removing restrictions on how many stations a given corporation could own. Clear Channel owns 1,200 stations nationally. As Molly Ivins writes in her column of July 28, 2002 (*Bloomington-Normal Pantagraph*),

> Clear Channel moves into a city and rents, say, a floor of a building, which is mostly a sales office but also has eight little closets for eight radio stations.
>
> The play list is shipped in from headquarters and is the same all over the country, for Top 40 or Easy Listening or country—we thus have less and less sense of our localities, of our regional music, fewer opportunities for new talent.

Is the answer to the problem presented by a monolithic corporate imagination to find new regulatory prescriptions in order to return to the good old days when corporations at least had to compete with each other? I don't think so. We need to be able to think and imagine something better and more ambitious than that.

Which brings me to the next part of my prescription. To get to a point where freedom and centrality for the imagination are possible and the kind of corporate culture represented by Clear Channel can be meaningfully confronted, we will also need thought. One of my primary contentions in this book will be that our fate is likely to be a fatality so long as what we most urgently need, thought, is strictly prohibited (because thinking is that boring thing that the talking heads on TV do) or is presented in a fraudulent form (again, that boring thing that the talking heads on TV do) or is quarantined to areas of national life where it is next to irrelevant (the universities, "think" tanks, and agencies where those boring people go when they're not busy being talking heads on TV). And yet, thought ought to be the *liveliest* thing we do, because it is necessarily about the possibility of change. The presence of real thought in the culture (in place of what we have, a show-biz confidence game overseen by media moguls) would keep us constantly on the edge of our collective seats with common interest and anticipation. Instead we endure a situation in which we are free to think and say what we like so long as what we think and say doesn't matter, doesn't threaten dominant state/corporate/military narratives. In a world dominated by Clear Channel, it is very difficult to say something large and loud enough that it might begin to matter. Not even Bill Moyers's increasingly radical and hostile PBS program, "NOW: With Bill Moyers," could be said to have sufficient viewers to matter. CNN and network news do matter, but they are utterly in line with two-party/corporate/militarist assumptions.

The opening up of public life to thought is not really different from the opening up of public life to the imagination. The two—thought and the imagination, philosophy and art—are at least complementary if not the same thing. Wallace Stevens referred to himself as a "philosopher's man." Today, even within universities (or maybe especially within universities), you can hardly find a poet who has something to say to a philosopher, and vice versa. By and large, the academic poet is a writer of lyrics. Poetry is all "occasional," stimulated by a local incident, or, at best, a very fragmented experience. Say what you will about T. S. Eliot's politics and poetry (and I've never liked either much), he took poetry's purview to be the world writ large. Our history. Our fate. That sort of hubris, that breadth of vision, is mostly absent in the world of poetry administered by organizations like the Associated Writing Programs. Poets are taught to write short, discrete poems, send them off to the little magazines, get tenure, and enjoy life. That's the poet's imperative. On the philosopher's side, it's all analytics. Departments of philosophy have fled their own traditions. The thinking of continental philosophy is mostly absent and mostly an embarrassment for our Anglo-American neo-positivists. Hegel, Kant, Heidegger, et al. can be found in English departments if they can be found at all. As a consequence, poets and philosophers, when they meet, can only look at each other mouths agape, stunned that such creatures should be. It's just another astonishing and depressing national dysfunction.

I would still maintain, unlikely though it is, that imagination and thought, art and philosophy, are the things we urgently need if we are ever to confront the performative logic, the imperatives to efficiency and domination, of our culture. I would go even further. Reawakening the imagination and a capacity for thought is a spiritual and perhaps even a mystical procedure. This has nothing to do with the crises of rising or falling church attendance at the corner Presbyterian church. Our spiritual crisis is human, historical, and social. What, we need to ask, is the spiritual content of a concept like justice? Ultimately, our crisis of the imagination is a crisis of spirit related to Henry James's notion of a moral individual. For James, the moral individual is "richly responsible and richly aware." But how is it possible to be aware and responsible in a society that prohibits understanding and grants all responsibility to governmental and commercial institutions?

What I would like to suggest is that art and thought can best confront these corporate realities, can best perform their social roles, by turning to a version of what Immanuel Kant called the "sublime." For Kant, the sublime arrives through "a presentation of the imagination which prompts much thought, but to which no determinate thought whatsoever, i.e. no *concept*, can be adequate." (181) One risk in thinking in these terms is that the sublime can lead to an idea of art that is mystified and removed from the human world, an art for art's sake. I can protect against this possibility only by providing the notion of the sublime, as I'd like to use it, with specific content. We need a practical and concrete sublime. A sublime for the here and now. As Hegel wrote in the preface to *Phenomenology of Spirit* (that most bewildered, uncanny, and sublime work of the philosophic imagination — so sublime, in fact, that it is written in a style that makes it seem as if Hegel feared to be understood), one does not begin philosophy with a definite notion of method. One begins by beginning. My models of the concrete sublime, then, are books without method, books that begin by beginning, that are not sure what they think, but think passionately and purposefully nevertheless against the administered world of the "automatic." These works of the concrete sublime are antagonists to the status quo in entertainment, intellectual orthodoxy, and political ideology. They are advocates for change, and they need to be much larger public presences.

Marshall McLuhan's *The Mechanical Bride* (1951) is a model work of the imagination and of the sublime. Unlike his later work, beginning with *The Gutenberg Galaxy* (1962), McLuhan's *The Mechanical Bride* has no explicit worldview. It has no buzz to sell. It offers nothing to the talk shows. Instead of preaching to the "new tribalism" or "electric culture" as he was later to do (in a most unsublime if not silly way), McLuhan provides only the sterling of his own critical and artistic performance. The sublime *is The Mechanical Bride* itself. It yearns for what it can't adequately express, and offers us as consolation the exemplary art of its own critical activities. It is a work we should honor for that reason.

McLuhan's only assertion in *The Mechanical Bride*, which I am happy to accept as the sole assertion of the present work, is that "[i]t is critical vision alone which can mitigate the unimpeded operation of the automatic." (87) Through this critical vision, "we are happily permitted some degree of critical reflection on other alternatives." (90)

This modest claim captures the fullness of the obligation to criticism and renewal through which the imagination must work. The imagination "happily permits" criticism and the creation of alternatives.

That is my purpose and the sum of my method in these pages.

Chapter 1

THE MIDDLE MIND

Having adapted Beethoven's Sixth Symphony for *Fantasia*,
Walt Disney commented: "Gee! This'll make Beethoven."
Marshall McLuhan

1.

I've suspected for some time that there's something missing in the way
we usually construct the Culture Wars. Bennett, Cheney, D'Souza,
Kimball, etc., on one side. Fish, Graff, Bérubé, Mapplethorpe, etc.,
on the other. I've been as involved and absorbed in this *faux* drama as
anyone, but at the same time, dimly, I have wondered: Do these characters really stand for things people care about? I mean, in places
other than the *Chronicle for Higher Education* and the *National Review?*

And then at last it occurred to me that this titanic agon was just a
diversion from the real action. There is another cultural politics in our
midst, perhaps even more organic than the academic left or ideological right. It is moving, making its way, accumulating its forces, *winning* while putative conservatives and tenured radicals beat the bloody
hell out of each other to no end at all. This third force I call our Middle Mind. It is a vast mind, my friends, and I fear it is already something towering and permanent on our national horizon.

The Middle Mind attempts to find a middle way between the ideological hacks of the right and of the theorized left. Unlike Middle-
brow, the Middle Mind does not locate itself between high and low
culture. Rather, it asserts its right to speak for high culture indifferent
to both the traditionalist right and the academic left.

The Middle Mind is pragmatic, plainspoken, populist, contemptuous of the right's narrowness, and incredulous before the left's convolutions. It is adventuresome, eclectic, spiritual, and in general agreement with liberal political assumptions about race, gender, and class. The Middle Mind really rather liked Bill Clinton, thoroughly supported his policies, but wished that the children didn't have to know so much about his personal life. The Middle Mind is liberal. It wants to protect the Arctic National Wildlife Refuge, and has bought an SUV with the intent of visiting it. It even understands in some indistinct way that that very SUV spells the Arctic's doom. Most important, the Middle Mind imagines that it honors the highest culture and that it lives through the arts. It supports the local public broadcasting station, supports the symphony, attends summer Shakespeare festivals, and writes letters to state representatives encouraging support for the state arts council. The Middle Mind's take on culture is well intended, but it is also deeply deluded.

One way or the other, what I'm here to tell you is that the Middle Mind is winning. That is, it has the most plausible claim to being the true representative of the public's opinion. Now, you might say, given the mostly liberal markers I have described above, that worse things could happen. That's true enough. We could be returned to William Bennett's puritanical world of culture as quasi-religious credo. Our "legacy," indistinguishable from our manacles. But however liberal its methods, the Middle Mind is still a form of management, and its final purpose, even if it's not a purpose it's aware of, is to assure that the imagination is not abroad, not out and about, and certainly not doing its own powerful thing.

I'd like to review a few recent exfoliations of the Middle Mind that have drifted by me. It's not always easy to know when one is in the presence of the Middle Mind. It generally flies below critique's radar, because it has the advantage of not being associated with a particular political camp. It feels "natural," which is how we can be pretty sure it's winning. It has its effect *and* passes notice. A neat trick in *Kulturkampf.*

The Middle Mind is very well connected. It doesn't need bags of money from conservative foundations and think tanks to create its presence. The Middle Mind is present effortlessly. It comes to us with the convincing and implicit claim, "You've been curious about this, you've been waiting for it, and wondering about it, and here it is." The Middle Mind is frequently on public TV *(Charlie Rose)*, in city weeklies, and in book review sections of slick magazines *(Spin* and *GQ)*. It is everywhere on National Public Radio, even shows like *Whad'Ya Know?* but our collective nose is rubbed in it on Terry Gross's *Fresh Air. Fresh Air* is not merely a promotional vehicle for the Middle Mind, it is itself a prime example of the Middle Mind in all its charm and banality.

Let's think about Terry Gross and *Fresh Air* with particular regard for her cultural programming. (I will have nothing to say here about her efforts in public affairs.) Here is an interview program that claims quite earnestly to be for intelligence, for the fresh and new, for something other than regular stale network culture, for the arts and for artists. But anyone who listens much to the show knows (I certainly hope that I'm not the only one who has noticed) that: a) Terry Gross has no capacity for even the grossest distinctions between artists and utter poseurs. (Many of the "writers" she has interviewed recently have been writers for TV series and movies. People who can with a straight face say, *"Seinfeld* is a great show because of the brilliant scriptwriting" love *Fresh Air.* Now, *Seinfeld* may be a cut above the average sitcom, but *it's a sitcom!*) b) The show is a pornographic farce.

Let me develop this last idea about the pornographic. Terry Gross's interest in books and writers is too often morbid, perverse, and voyeuristic. Two quick examples: in 2001 she interviewed Alan Ball, the writer of the HBO series *Six Feet Under.* The critical moment in the interview came when she asked him (I'm paraphrasing), "What was it like when you were in that car accident and your sister was driving and she died but you didn't?" Was she leading up to a telling psychological reading of the work in question? No. She wanted to know (and I suspect her audience wanted to know) *what it was like to be in an auto accident in which his sister died!* That's it. Do we learn something about writing, or the arts, or culture? Do we learn *anything?* Only that he was traumatized by the event.

And what are the folks who go on this show thinking, knowing that they'll face this kind of personal inquisition? They're probably thinking either, *"Fresh Air!* The big time!" Or "Good grief, that show is a joke. But my publicist will shoot me if I don't do it."

A week or so after the Alan Ball interview there was a program in which Gross interviewed the writer Carol Muske-Duke, author of the novel *Life After Death.* In this novel, a woman says, "Drop dead," to her husband and the next day he does. Before the novel was published, the author's own real-life husband died on a tennis court. *This* was the point at which the book became interesting for Gross. If Muske-Duke's poor husband hadn't dropped dead, Gross would never have been interested in her or her book for this Show of Shows. "What did it feel like to suspect you'd killed your own husband with your art?" *Fresh Air?* How about Lurid Speculations? It's like Dr. Laura for people with bachelor's degrees. *Car Talk* has more intellectual content.

There are, alas, all too many examples of this kind. I occasionally time Gross's interviews with artists to see how long she can go before taking her "turn to the personal." (And why is it, I might ask, that she makes this turn with artists only? Why doesn't she make the same turn with guests brought on to discuss social and political issues? Is it because she has some sort of assumption that art is finally about autobiographical confession? All art seems to be a sort of tawdry memoir for her.) In early 2002, she was interviewing the artist Frank Stella and things were going along okay, things weren't too bad, when—wham! "Hey, Frank, what's up with the mangled hand?" Stella's response dripped with indifference, but Gross persisted. "I mean, like, how'd it happen, dude?"

The truth of her vaunted technique was revealed in a 2002 interview of Gross by Ira Glass. Glass asked, essentially, "Well, how do you get people to reveal things about themselves if they don't want to?" And Terry replied, taking the question perfectly seriously, as if Glass were getting to the heart of the mystery of her craft, "Oh, sometimes it's pretty hard to get them to reveal things they don't want to reveal." When Gross interviewed Gene Simmons of Kiss, who proceeded to astonish the country with his vulgar and macho self-revelations, the only thing unusual about the interview was that Simmons was all too happy to bare all and then some. That's been his stock-in-trade for three decades. He's good at it. Unwittingly, he also allowed Gross to reveal *Fresh Air*'s real strength: its host is a schlock jock.

From the perspective of a person really interested in art and culture, one can only say, "Well, she says she's on my side, but, God, she's so stupidly on my side that I hardly recognize my side as my side." Thus the Middle Mind.

As I've considered various avatars of the Middle Mind, I've occasionally felt that my criticisms were a bit unseemly or even unkind. Terry Gross. Isn't she probably a very nice person? Good companion? Probably picks up the tab for lunch more than her share of the time and doesn't complain if you had a couple of drinks. Of my next instance, however, one need have no such reservations, because Joe Queenan's *Balsamic Dreams* (2001) is one of the nastiest books I've read in some time. The rightwing character assassin has nothing on this guy.

Queenan's thesis is not deceptively simple. It's just simple. And familiar. Simple and familiar used to equal trite, but the Middle Mind has infused the trite with a new vigor. Queenan argues that Baby Boomers are a failed generation, largely because of their overwhelming obsession with "me." Queenan has little to add to the usual conservative critique of the Me Generation except the novel observation that what's most wrong about the obsession with "me" is that it's "annoying." "Decent folk," he explains, are "annoyed" by Boomer cars, jobs, money, music, self-referential conversation, hypocritical moralizing, and lack of self-awareness. Leave it to a Boomer, as Queenan confesses he is, to base a moral judgment on the never-defined term "annoying." Annoying to whom? Queenan and "decent folk"?

But exactly who, one might ask, ever manages to be "decent" in Queenan's worldview? Queenan makes it clear that it is not Tom

Brokaw's "Greatest Generation" of World War II, which he finds to be a sad embarrassment, and Generation X is no better at all than its Boomer parents. So, were the decent people all born before 1920? Should we imagine a lot of annoyed octogenarians tottering around? Seriously, given Queenan's methods, it would be a miracle if he ever found a single decent person.

Of course, this ethos constructed of that-which-annoys is itself very annoying. The greatest annoyance proper to *Balsamic Dreams* itself is its persistent willingness to contend that it means anything at all to generalize about generations. Perhaps one should say, "What goes around comes around" (to use one of the Boomerisms that Queenan hates so much). *Balsamic Dreams* is Ginsberg's *Howl* in full retreat. But Ginsberg at least had the wisdom to see that the mammon he howled against was not the responsibility of any one generation. I'd happily join Queenan in a good old-fashioned rant against humanity as such, as Philip Wylie does in *A Generation of Vipers*, Twain did before him, and Swift did before Twain. But that wouldn't have the buzz and commercial hook that bashing Boomers has. And it wouldn't get him on *Fresh Air*.

> *Terry:* "*Do you really dislike your own generation because it likes balsamic vinegar?*"

Quel scandal! How interesting, fresh, and utterly Middle Mind. (Why can't Queenan admit that balsamic vinaigrette tastes better than that thousand-island crap made out of mayonnaise and pickle relish that we had to eat on iceberg lettuce in the fifties?)

A few last comments on Queenan: Since when do we have to put up with ethical diatribes from columnists for *GQ*? Is that where all the decent folk have gone? They're all at *GQ*? Why isn't *GQ* an expression of Boomer culture? Do they all eschew balsamic vinaigrette at *GQ*?

Ironically, the ultimate retort to my critique of *Balsamic Dreams* could very well be that my thesis about the Middle Mind simply confirms Queenan's propositions about Boomers, because the Middle

Mind is what you get when Boomers take over culture. Okay, Joe, I get it. Good job.

The Middle Mind is also interested in the spiritual, but not in the right wing's Christian fundamentalist spirituality-with-teeth. By and large, the Middle Mind is in pursuit of the Buddha. Books that seek to explain Buddhism or introduce it to North Americans are a large and growing publishing phenomenon making certain spiritual leaders, such as Thich Nhat Hahn (the Vietnamese Buddhist teacher of "mindfulness"), into something approaching international celebrities. (Mindfulness, by the way, is not a product of the Middle Mind. No. We actually could use that capacity, although we won't get it through the Middle Mind.) One of the hottest such books in recent years was Dinty W. Moore's *The Accidental Buddhist* (1999). It is a mostly chronological description of the author's experiences and reflections on what he calls "my American Buddhism project":

> Then I had this bright idea—the best way to learn about Bud-
> dhism would be to see it in action, the best way to imagine
> how it might fit into my hectic life would be to see how other
> Americans are fitting it into their busy American lives. I was
> always a big fan of quests of adventures, and here was a
> chance to have my own. (19)

Several things make *The Accidental Buddhist* an example of the Middle Mind:

- The author is apparently convinced that his audience doesn't know anything about Buddhism and wouldn't be able to distinguish its proponents from Hare Krishna panhandlers at an airport. (By the way, what happened to those guys?—a national consequence of the great Giuliani cleanup?) The Middle Mind assumes that the people it takes as its audience don't know anything; it assumes that most people are benevolently stupid: "Oh, Buddhism. Tell me about that."

- The book is written in the kind of prose that works in a made-for-TV novel: "About this time, an auburn-haired, distinctly beautiful young woman walks by in the sort of exceedingly tight red dress that can make a man's heart do the hokeypokey." (45)

- No one, least of all the author, is required to think. Any genuine intellectual content attaching to Buddhism is apologized for both directly ("Understand? I'm not sure *I* do, frankly" [50] or "Whew, it does get deep" [156]) and through a down-dumbing trivialization ("Why Do Tibetans Have Such Trouble with Their Vacuum Cleaners?"[39]). Frederick Streng's book on Mahayana philosophy, *Emptiness: A Study in Religious Meaning,* is a great work of intellect about a subject which has an intellectual aspect. *The Accidental Buddhist* is not such a book, nor *could* it be since its aspirations are closely limited by the managers of the Middle Mind (in this case, the editorial staff at Main Street Books, a division of Doubleday). By the way, and this is a large part of my point, Streng's book is long out-of-print. Of course.

But once one recognizes what kind of mind it is that one is dealing with (a middling mind, as I have said), we can acknowledge that this mind is making a good-faith effort to report on something that is in fact very important. This is the frustrating thing about the Middle Mind. Joe Queenan is not wrong to condemn yuppies (whoever they are) who walk their dogs while talking on cell phones from their slowly rolling SUVs. (I have to say, though, that this sounds an awful lot like the sort of apocryphal myth Reagan used to spin about "welfare cheats"; it's Reagan's technique turned the other way. Have *you* ever seen someone walk his dog, cell phone in hand, from a rolling SUV?) And Dinty Moore is not wrong to pass along to us the words of Bhante Gunaratana:

You suffer from the same malady that infects every human being. It is a monster inside all of us, and it has many arms; chronic tension, lack of genuine compassion for others, including the people closest to you, feelings being blocked up, and emotional deadness. . . . We build a whole culture around hiding from it, pretending it is not there, and distracting ourselves from it with goals and projects and status. But it never goes away. It is a constant undercurrent in every thought and every perception; a little wordless voice at the back of the head that keeps saying, "Not good enough yet. Got to have more. Got to make it better. Got to be better." (120)

The Accidental Buddhist is not a horrible book and it is certainly not a good book. It cannot hurt Buddhism, although it's hard to see how it might help it (except insofar as it might lead someone to seek a truly good book about Buddhism). My contention is simply that a mediocre book—facilitated by a culture of mediocrity that forbids real intelligence—hurts us all.

One of the most common gambits of the Middle Mind is to claim to provide high culture while really providing something a good deal less. Thus, one of the unspoken assumptions of *Fresh Air* is that "some of our best writers work for TV." Queenan and Moore provide a sociology and theology perfectly appropriate to the expectations and conceptual capacities of the readers of *Time* magazine. The Middle Mind's motto could be "Promise him culture but give him TV."

There is no lack of subjects for an essay on the Middle Mind. Perhaps, for example, you've noticed that *Antiques Road Show* has turned arts and antiquities into crude commodity fetishism:

> *Expert antiquarian: "This spittoon embossed with the crest of the House of Summersoft is worth $4,000, top dollar at auction."*
>
> *Pallid owner: "Ooh! I had no idea!"*
>
> *Pallid owner thinks: "I could sell this now and have that money, but then I wouldn't have the spittoon, and I'd probably just spend the money on some sort of crap, and after a while the thing I bought will be indistinguishable from all the other things I've bought, things I didn't buy*

*with this special free money from the implausibly valuable spittoon, and
then I won't remember it was special at all, because I bought it with this
money, this spittoon money, and so I'll have nothing, really, not even the
spittoon. But what's the point of keeping the spittoon? Is it the pleasure of
knowing I could turn it into cash any time I liked, if I wanted? Or maybe
I should actually spit in it once in a while. This smart man says that
Queen Victoria probably once spat in it. Or is it spit? Spitted? No. Ooh,
I'm so confused."*

2.

Shortly after the first appearance of "The Middle Mind," in *Context*
and the "Readings" section of *Harper's* in 2002, I discovered a clever
book by *New Yorker* staff writer John Seabrook called *Nobrow: The
Culture of Marketing, the Marketing of Culture. Nobrow* contends
with many of the same issues that I try to come to terms with in the
concept of the Middle Mind. Seabrook's work, however, is a critique
of the Middle Mind written from *within* the Middle Mind. Let's see
what that looks like.

Seabrook's thesis, as the book's jacket copy captures accurately, is:

> In the old days, highbrow was elite and unique and lowbrow
> was commercial and mass-produced. These distinctions have
> been eradicated by a new cultural landscape where "serious"
> artists show their work at Kmart, *Titanic* becomes a best-
> selling classical album, and Roseanne Barr guest edits *The
> New Yorker*: in short, a culture of Nobrow.

Even if we put aside the extreme likelihood that any book that can
accurately capture its argument in a jacket blurb is not likely to be a
good book, *Nobrow* provides other compelling reasons to conclude
that it is crummy cultural criticism:

- Like a lot of trade books on culture (Queenan's *Balsamic Dreams* and *Bobos in Paradise* by David Brooks are good examples), *Nobrow* has only one idea (highbrow/lowbrow has been replaced by Nobrow), which Seabrook develops through variation, repetition, and example without ever creating a general argument, especially an argument for whether the Nobrow phenomenon is a good or bad thing. He proceeds with more neutrality than scientists describing changing climate patterns (although even climatologists are inclined these days to say, "Hey, it's seventy-five degrees in Minneapolis in January. Is anybody bothered by this?"). If I were pressed to describe Seabrook's politics, I'd say that he gives the impression that Nobrow is a mostly bad thing that nevertheless rocks his world (as Nobrow might put it). In short, the book is conceptually gruel-thin.

- If someone wondered what "bicoastal arrogance" was about, *Nobrow* could answer all the questions. For Seabrook, it's not even about complete coasts. It's not even about all of Manhattan. For Seabrook, the world runs in a triangle from midtown (from the old *New Yorker* office to MTV's studio at Forty-fourth Street) to record producer David Geffen's house in LA to the White House (when Bill Clinton was in it). That's what counts in the world according to Seabrook. (Okay, I lied: Seabrook describes one road trip slumming in Austin.)

- Seabrook contends that "by the 1990s the notion that high culture constituted some sort of superior reality, and that people who made it were superior beings, was pretty much in the toilet." (70) Of course, Seabrook's calendar is ludicrous. The Culture Industry drove a stake in highbrow forty years earlier. (Actually, the stake was driven into highbrow's brow, effectively pithing it, as you'd do with a frog in biology. Highbrow was thus rendered present but insensate.) Pop art displaced high art through cinema, rock 'n' roll, and the School of Warhol in the mid-1960s. Of course, these facts are not convenient to Seabrook's need to be able to claim that this is all new, he's on the edge, giving us the scoop, and reading this book is all part of being "in the house" with those who should know. How's he going to capture a little buzz if he's talking about something really old, like something that happened before 1990?

- Seabrook has the annoying habit of being sycophantic to the very people he ought to be judging critically. Tina Brown made the *New Yorker* Nobrow, but she's "brilliant" anyway. David Geffen is a man of "exquisite sensitivity to pop-cultural fads" (for Seabrook, that's a good thing). George Lucas's *Star Wars* is "our classic." *Nobrow* is a book by an insider taking an intellectual vacation on the outside but being very careful not to burn any bridges because *he's going back*. And he knows it. (Of course, one could argue that the idea that *Nobrow* ever really leaves the inside is one of its primary fictions. Seabrook isn't writing criticism, he's inside creating content; he's making a product.) In a March 2002 issue of the *New Yorker*, Seabrook is back at his desk writing about designer Yeohlee Teng's attempts to create fashionable nursing uniforms. Seabrook happily plies the Nobrow world of cultural criticism indistinguishable from ad copy and gossip columns.

- *Nobrow*'s greatest flaw as cultural criticism is that it resolutely refuses to think. (The box containing the products of the Middle Mind is always cheerfully marked in bright letters, NO THINKING REQUIRED! as if that were the final blandishment needed in order to convince us to make that fateful purchase.) Seabrook asserts, "Highbrow/lowbrow has been replaced by Nobrow." Are those the only terms in which to think about this problem, Mr. Seabrook? "I'm not goin' there," he replies. But surely our options can't be limited to submit to Nobrow or try hopelessly to return to highbrow. Is that really it? C'mon, let's think together. "I said, I'm not dealing with that. I've got editors, you know. An advance is at risk here—a very nice advance, thank you. And I already spent most of it on an Ermenegildo Zegna suit." Seabrook is looking a little pale and panicky. But what did the counterculture represent for you?

Or punk? Or autonomous "folk" culture, what you call the "little grid"? Is there no authentic independent culture worth talking about as an alternative to Nobrow? Are there no options here save abject capitulation? Then Seabrook does that *Play It Again, Sam* Woody Allen routine where he's got his hands over his ears and he's screaming crazily and pacing around so that he can't hear what's being said.

Although it is not good cultural criticism, it is, oddly enough, a very interesting novel.[1] The plot is simple, as befits a *New Yorker* writer. It even has a little epiphany of self-realization without which the *New Yorker* story would be even less than the nothing it is. The only character is one John Seabrook, an earnest, intelligent young man confronted by a fraud which he understands as only an insider can, and in great and telling detail. He is a modern Candide. The perceptive and innocent protagonist proceeds in episodic fashion by scenes of travesty, fraud, greed, and violence. Patron whoring. Substitution of brand recognition for evaluation of quality. A world of "worthless time-wasting hacks." Caliban casts out Ariel. MTV promotes the murderous, misogynistic worldview of gangsta rap. As a novel, *Nobrow* is about the tension between critique and submission. The narrative hook is, "When will our hero turn on all this? When will he condemn it? When will he distance himself morally from a world he knows to be soulless?" As the book progresses, the reader becomes increasingly worried. Seabrook creates the same sort of unease that you feel when confronted by the wealthy rock 'n' roll heroin addict who says, "Hey, I can afford the dope, so what's the problem?"

And all you want to say is, "Yeah, but it's not very good for you, is it?"

---

[1] The perspicacious reader may have already noted that the present work is of uncertain genre and may in fact itself be a novel of some kind.

Most painful of all, Seabrook reveals that MTV stages its "authentic" live-music scenes by putting the "attractive-looking" kids in front where the camera and the viewer will see only their bodacious bods, dreds, and tatted-tits. In a rush, all of our memories of not being the attractive kids well up in us, and the resentment grows, that familiar old resentment against the in-crowd, and we think, "He won't let this pass. This goes too far. We know John Seabrook. He wasn't one of the 'attractive kids.' He read books like we did. He'll do the right thing." But the moment passes and not a mumblin' word is said. And then we're all of us falling through the floor of the culture, like the suburban houses sinking into graveyards in the movie *Poltergeist*, engulfed by the shit produced by the modern Culture Industry. But Seabrook looks on from the edge of the disaster, the last sellout standing. The fact is that he's personally more powerful because of this disaster. He's aloof and above it all. He's slamming a power drink. (No, it's not Gatorade. He's got a new product because he's in every test-marketing survey. He's got the newest of the new power drinks with the synthetic adrenal gland stimulants with the psycho-active hookup, sort of like a triple espresso sweetened with Power Gel and a little dose of Ecstasy for good measure. This is the drink that gives you the virtual experience of a Jordan sky-dunk even as you crash to the floor of the emergency ward.) He's Candide in extremis, a feckless voyeur standing on the cusp of our shared disaster.

Seabrook's book is the first fully realized novel of what French social critic Jean Baudrillard called "the ecstasy of communication." Baudrillard argued that the real is gone, and we have only the simulacrum (imitation, fraud) in its place. There is no possibility of returning to the authentic, but why should we even want to? Capitulating to the flow of signs and consumer goods is sexy, euphoric, ecstatic. So let the flow flow. Feel it. Mmmm, *Star Wars*. Mmmm, fucking Rita Brown. Give it to me with that Geffen-take on what's hot. But keep what's not hot hence, cuz that's foe to man. Seabrook capitulates to "the buzz." He's got that Nobrow buzz thang goin' on. He's got the hip-hop stocking cap, Discman to the ears, and he's the illest, groovin' down to MTV to chill with the global homies.[2]

It's like the logic of "how I stopped worrying and learned to love the bomb." Seabrook argues, in essence, "Okay, if you're Old School, there are some little issues with authenticity and quality and stuff. And I admit that most of this crap is crap. But what's authentic? I mean, show me. I am *not* going to listen to Haydn string quartets, so just forget it. I'm a smart guy and a good writer—sort of an *artist*, you might say—and I'm happy living in World World. I'm happy with the life of the Corporate Imagination. MTV works for me. If this is The End of History, worse things could happen, believe me." Seabrook is Odysseus self-submitted to the Sirens, but he forgot to tell someone to tie him down. He has jumped out of the damned boat, he's swimming toward the Sirens, and he yells back at us, "See you later, suckers!"

Our "novel" leaves Seabrook (this is his little *New Yorker* epiphany that we've been waiting for) "in Times Square shivering under the skyscraper in which the last of [*New Yorker* publisher] William Shawn's notions about editorial independence would be entombed." He had "reached Nobrow ground zero, the exact midpoint at which culture and marketing converged." (213)

Differently said, as Ezra Pound put it at the time of World War I, "a tawdry cheapness shall outlast our day." Now that's an epiphany appropriate to our moment.

3.

The Middle Mind is able to accomplish its business in part, as I have said, because its assumptions have become so naturalized. In the world of the Middle Mind, all one asks of art is that it be "entertaining,"

---

[2] Don't even start with the crap about the Middle Mind buzz. The Middle Mind is straight dope.

"fun," and "interesting," and that's as it should be. Things are "interesting" in the Middle Mind in much the same way that a character would be said to be "clever" in a novel by Henry James. For James, a clever person has all of the appearance of perceptiveness without really being perceptive at all.

And so we can say that the PBS documentary sagas of Ken Burns (*Baseball, The Civil War, Mark Twain,* etc.) are "interesting," while in fact the material has almost no intellectual consequence beyond being entertaining and blandly informative. Burns refuses to question the nature of historical narration, presents chronology and facts as beyond question (as if facts were little nuggets that you could pick up and put in your pocket), while allowing "experts" like Congressional Representative Stuart Symington to wax indulgent and sentimental over the meaning and pathos of the Civil War, quoting Rudyard Kipling, of all people. The idea that "history is the story of events as told by the victors" would seem scandalous and cynical to Burns. This is not a point of view that he would allow in his work. He rarely even allows a truly dissident voice into his programs. (It was a genuine surprise and relief to hear James Baldwin say, in the recently rebroadcast Burns documentary "Statue of Liberty," that to black Americans the Statue of Liberty means absolutely nothing but a testimony to hypocrisy; it was as if someone who had been suffocating was suddenly allowed to take a breath of air.)[3] Burns's programs always end with the banjos playing or Coplandish strings sighing out something truly sentimental and finally fraudulent.

With expectations no greater than being entertaining, fun, and interesting, a filmmaker like Steven Spielberg—a Middle Mind artist if

---

[3] According to Sasha Abramsky quoting the Sentencing Project in the *Chronicle for Higher Education,* November 15, 2002, "About 12 percent of African-American men in their 20's are in jail or prison in America, and, in some Southern states, close to 1 percent of the total population . . . are now imprisoned." If these prisoners are in a "third strike" state, they could be doing consecutive life sentences for crimes equivalent to lunch money for Enron crooks. They're making license plates or whatever, mostly without meaningful compensation, and generally wondering if them cotton fields back home weren't really the good old days. So, statue of what?

ever there was one—can achieve and sustain a reputation that makes his work appear different from and bigger than the rote productions of the Hollywood system. He's above that, it's generally thought. His films are major national and international events. But the Middle Mind couldn't survive, and Steven Spielberg couldn't survive, reputation intact, if they were confronted by a populace that was capable of reading well.

For instance, a few years ago we had the opportunity to see Spielberg's much-lauded movie *Saving Private Ryan*, a movie that returned us to a certain narrative ground—the war saga set in the battlefields of Europe during World War II—for what seemed like the first time since Burt Lancaster and company put all of those hoary conventions emphatically to rest in the surreal *Castle Keep*. Since the events surrounding 9-11 and the rebirth of jingoistic patriotism on these shores, the assumptions of *Saving Private Ryan* have become something like national legal tender. Because of this film, old memorials to the War are being burnished and new ones are being built. Worse yet, this film has played an important part in the broad propaganda effort that legitimizes our current thinking about the necessity and usefulness of war in places such as Iraq.[4] But what might our conclusions about this film be, what might our considerations of Spielberg as an artist be, if we were to seriously consider the narrative structure of this film? I ask this question because I don't believe that most movie viewers think seriously about what's being presented to them in films like *Saving Private Ryan*, and I'd like to know how actually thinking through such art would change how we think about these films, change the enormous

---

[4] As with past administrations, portraying military excursions as "like World War II" is a favorite rhetorical gambit of the present Bush administration. In August of 2002, Vice President Cheney outraged the Western world community when he compared Iraq to Nazi Germany and President Bush to Winston Churchill. The outrage was not inappropriate, but a good laugh might have been more productive. After all, it was the eloquent and statesman-like Bush who once said, memorably (as quoted in *Talk*, September 1999), "Nobody needs to tell me what I believe. But I do need somebody to tell me where Kosovo is."

presence of the Middle Mind, and change, finally, what we expect
from art and what we want in this world of ours.

I have discussed this movie with several distinct groups of friends
as have many viewers of the film, both in the privacy of our homes and
on the messy public airwaves of "talk radio." I have been surprised that
my friends—intelligent, sophisticated people on the whole—had no
idea what I was talking about when I elaborated my understanding of
the film's "lesson." At one level, as the film's title announces, it is about
the last surviving son of a family and the heroic efforts of a platoon of
American soldiers to find him and return him safely to his mother. But
at a second level, *Private Ryan* is about a command not to kill a German prisoner who then returns to kill Americans, most notably the
heroic Captain Miller. Thus the movie's frightening lesson (one that
I've come to think of as archetypally North American) is: always
choose death, for if you do not, death will come anyway, later, multi-
plied.

When I called my friends' attention to the fact that Spielberg had
chosen to have the initial decision not to kill made by a multilingual
intellectual (and coward!), their response was usually along the lines
of "What's Spielberg got to do with the fact that he was a coward?"; "I
didn't like that guy"; "He was spineless." What I finally had to con-
clude was that while I was treating the character of the intellectual
Upham as a part of Spielberg's artifice, as an important element in an
artistic structure, which structure once in place could be asked to reveal its meaning (and perhaps Spielberg's ideological baggage), my
friends saw these characters as . . . real people. They understood them
in the same way that they understood the cashiers who sold them their
tickets and popcorn out front. Upham was a coward in the same way
that the snack bar cashier was a little on the chubby side.

In short, my ominous conclusion was that they didn't know how to
"read" the film. That is to say, they didn't know how to abstract the in-
tegument of structure from a piece of narrative art in order to begin to
talk about how the thing *means* (i.e., creates an ethical world).

And if my intelligent, art-savvy friends didn't know how to do this, what was going on with all of the blunt teenage receptors (mostly boys) that filled the theater on the evening that I first saw the movie? "BOOM!"[5] Was that it? Or should I have worried that the message about the imperative to choose death was also at some subpineal level oozing in and around their minds?

And where does Spielberg fit in all this? Is he a sort of modern-day Albert Speer? A brilliant technician in the service of sinister ideals? Or is he just mouthing a bunch of dumb platitudes and aping conventional gestures with no more awareness of the meanings his story creates than his bluntly receptored audience has?

All of which is to say that a simple movie-going experience is in fact a problem of both political and literary scope. What does it mean when the most sinister ideological notions pass virtually without comment in mass culture narratives because the audience is not interested in deciphering (or does not know how to decipher) what is in the film? Worse yet, what does it mean when these essentially unread artifacts are then blandly taken up by the instruments of the Middle Mind as America's art?

When I am asked, strolling away from the cineplex, whether I "liked" one of these heirs to cinematic art, I invariably say, "Yes, I liked it," or "No, I didn't like it," whatever aesthetic force my "liking" might have. But I also feel rather dumb about acknowledging a world in which liking or not-liking are my only options. When we capitulate in this way, aren't we just saying we're no better than Beavis and Butthead? This sucks, that rocks, this is awesome, and everything is just finally a lot stupid. Of course, this is a perfect state of affairs for the culture of the Middle Mind, which thrives on the thoughtless and ephemeral enthusiasms that it presents as culture.

---

[5] Marshall McLuhan has a great take in *The Mechanical Bride* on these young chaps for whom "boom" is enough. "Every day he gets beaten into a servile pulp by his own mechanical reflexes, which are constantly busy registering and reacting to the violent stimuli which his big, noisy, kinesthetic environment has provided for his unreflective reception." (79–80)

For a literate culture that understands that our narratives do serve to construct what we are, what our "content" is, and that trusts that the citizens to this culture know in some ultimate way what it means to read so that we may have some basis for moving among narrative options, this all implies a crisis of proverbially nightmarish proportions (oh, a quiet crisis, to be sure, in between the simulated explosions of mortar shells and other forms of synthetic, orgasmic, cinematic bliss). But without the self-consciousness that reading provides, we cannot *think* our culture, we can only be thought by it. In short, being able to read is a large part of what it means to be human as opposed to being a mere social function.

So, I'm going to "read" *Saving Private Ryan*. I think a reading can expose this film for what it is, a crypto-fascist work of historical revision. It's not even revision. It's a retrieval from a very dark place. It's: "Remember what we used to think? About patriotism? The glory of war? Let's think that again, and really mean it, so that it will be harder than hell to dislodge next time." Which is to say, this is a very dangerous movie.

Opening Credits. DreamWorks. A little boy perched on a crescent moon, fishing. Suggestions of Huck Finn and Walt Disney. In fact, thinking of Spielberg as our latter-day Walt Disney is revealing. Both men have been responsible for providing our national fantasy so that we aren't bothered by the obligation to have imaginations ourselves. Why be bothered with the nonproductive work of fantasy when the Unca Walts of the world can do it for us and stay neatly inside the ideological lines? By the way, has anyone seen Walt's cryogenicized corpse recently? I'm not implying anything. Just asking.

The American Flag. The first and last images in this movie are of the American flag, translucent, brilliant, rippling in the wind.

How are we to understand this flag? Why is it in the movie? Is it ironic? I'll just go ahead and tell you—no, it's not ironic. Nothing in this film undercuts or asks us to think about the flag's traditional, weepy appeal. This movie is yet another announcement of the death of sixties-style thought. This is not *Zabriskie Point*, not *Slaughterhouse Five*, not *Catch-22*, and certainly not *Castle Keep*. This is *The Big Chill*, take .

Or is the flag present in this movie because, well, flags are always in WWII movies? Is it a purely generic concession? That would be really stupid, if that's the case. It therefore very possibly *is* the case.

Opening Scene. Normandy. The aging WWII vet totters toward the grave of . . . we know not whom. Behind him comes his family. There's something interesting about this family. What the camera most encourages us to see is the three granddaughters, in their late teens, arm-in-arm, blonde, sweaters stretched over large (but not improperly large), round breasts. Ooh, they are well-titted, these little American wonders. They are the fruits of victory. Here, the answer to the film's purported "big" question, "Have I led a good life?" is answered. Hell yes. Look at these blonde babes my genes have launched. It's Aryan eugenics hybridized with Hollywood's sense of the good life. If the Nazis had won, and Hitler had settled down in Burbank, he wouldn't have thought any different.

My emphasis on the function of these beautiful young girls may seem perverse. Obviously, they don't play a large role in the movie. But I would insist that this film, like any novel, is an artifice. If there's something in it, it's there as a matter of artistic choice. The question then becomes, Why did Spielberg choose to have blonde, large-breasted granddaughters standing behind old-man Ryan as he asks the movie's putative big question? Is it because if there had to be girls in the film they might as well add to the general "beauty" of the product by contributing nice bazooms? Perhaps. This cynical, commercial, Hollywood-generic answer is certainly very plausible. Or is it, as I would also contend, that the girls are an implicit answer to the question that has no explicit answer, "Did I live a good life?" Think how the resonance of this question would change if Ryan had returned to Normandy alone. Or if he had gone only with an ill-kempt and frowsy wife without evidence of handsome offspring. Or what if the daughters had had lip and nose piercings and punk-blue hair? One way or the other, the response to the presence of the girls that is inadmissible is "It just happened that he had granddaughters with nice blonde hair and hand-some chests. So what?" The "so what" is that those girls are *not* his granddaughters. They came from casting central, to which they were admitted in the first place because, in large part, of their Hollywood-appropriate bosoms and lovely locks. Consequently, we ought to con-clude that they are present for two reasons. They are a Hollywood tautology (Hollywood movies have Hollywood-looking women in them), and they answer the narrative question, "Have I lived a good life?"

The Flashback. We look into the still-nameless vet's eyes. They take us back to the beach. Omaha Beach. Tom Hanks as Captain John Miller.

This is a brilliant moment. One has to pause and admire Spiel-berg's shrewdness. First, casting Hanks (a notorious softy) in this role was extraordinarily smart. He softens all the hard edges of this "war film." He reassures us that this will not be another *Pork Chop Hill* or *Ballad of the Green Berets*. Sure, Spielberg remembers Vietnam. He wouldn't make some macho war flick. Hanks is no John Wayne. Therefore, the film cannot be another VFW flack-piece. Shrewd.

Also, there is the narrative stratagem, the sleight of hand. We move from the eyes of the old man (who is in fact Private Ryan) to the viewpoint of Captain Miller (which Ryan could not possibly know). This is inspired cheating! Through it Spielberg maintains the narra-tive question: Who is the old man? This is very deft narrative manipu-lation.

The Landing. Truly horrific. These first minutes of the film are visu-ally stunning. War's horror (or a techno-wizard's version thereof) is re-ally captured. The claustrophobia of the landing boats and the water. The slaughter of the good guys into whose angular faces we had just been looking. These are authentic American faces right out of

Dorothea Lange's Farm Security Administration photographs of the 1930s. In a time like our own when the next generation of country boys and urban boys, our "volunteers," line up in order to take their part in the next mechanized slaughter (of little brown men, mostly, from Iraq or some other land-of-little-brown-people), this could be the opening of a morally engaging movie about the violence of war.

But it's not.

The tableau of the beach scene is stunning. Beautiful to see on the screen. Kubrick-like in its grandeur. Incongruous, too, given what has just preceded it. These men and machines integrated with the green and blue of nature. As the Italian Futurists used to say, "The deaths do not matter as long as the gesture is beautiful."

I think that just about every American movie expresses the conviction that there's something beautiful about death, especially violent death. It's in depicting death that our cinema can most be said to have a style. Violent death is our primary super-aesthetic. This is true even of oughta-know-better directors such as Martin Scorsese (as his epic study in urban carnage *Gangs of New York* has recently confirmed), and it's certainly true of the ragtag rest.[6]

The Plot. A platoon is sent behind enemy lines to rescue the last of four brothers, three of whom have already been killed in action. Some

---

[6] To this I would add only one other super-aesthetic: the striptease. It used to be that an American movie had to have a romantic angle. Now it must have a striptease. When the viewer sees the leading female actor early in the movie (Penelope Cruz in *Vanilla Sky*, Nicole Kidman and a cast of thousands in *Eyes Wide Shut*, etc.), he knows that there is a near certainty that at some point in the film he will have the pleasure of seeing her breasts (and if he's really lucky, her butt, too). It's nearly obligatory now. When *Twin Peaks* became the movie *Fire Walk with Me*, sure enough, Laura Palmer's bared breasts were suddenly part of the package. The hot news in January of 2003 was that the cast of TV's *Friends* would make a movie in 2004 . . . with nudity. All one can say is, "Of course. Why else would anyone want to see the execrable thing?" How spectacularly dull and predictable and insulting it has become. I acknowledge, however, that there are no leading ladies in *Saving Private Ryan* and so no leading-lady breasts to bare. We'll have to be satisfied with the granddaughters.

guy who looks frighteningly like Bob Dole playing General George C. Marshall reads a letter written by Abe Lincoln and everybody breaks down in tears and hysterics of patriotism and love of mother. Never mind that the letter doesn't make any sense in the context. In fact, because Lincoln's letter is about the loss of *all* of one unfortunate mother's sons, lost in the Civil War, Marshall ought to be encouraging the mother to say, "Well, hell, take the last one too. On that fucking glorious field of battle you talk about so purtily."

Forget this plot. It's a red herring. A sentimental red herring, if such a thing can be imagined. It's a cover for the real story.

The First Execution. Early in the movie, immediately after the Allies take the beachhead at Omaha, two surrendering Germans, hands held high, are shot by two American soldiers.

> Soldier 1: *"What did he say?"*
> Soldier 2: *"Look, I washed for supper."*

This cynical and murderous moment is of course the companion to the critical moment later in the film when Upham intervenes in the execution of the German prisoner. Writers pair similar moments in narrative in order to make clear their intentions, emphasize a theme, or provide self-commentary. How does the light of this first scene— which is disturbing in its cynicism and callousness—help us to understand Spielberg's moral purpose in the second and central execution?

The Second Execution. This scene (a depiction of a desperate human clinging to the threads of his life) is as well delivered by the actor Joerg Stadler as any in memory since John Turturro's *tour de force* performance in *Miller's Crossing*. The actor brilliantly captures the idea of the Enemy-Other-as-Human. His pathetic attempt to render "The Star-Spangled Banner": "I say can you see." Upham successfully argues that the German should be allowed to live. One sees the moral rightness of Upham's argument. After all, what they proposed was murder. The German was a POW and had certain rights under international law. Upham knew this. Surely, murder was not what the USA was about.

What allows Upham's argument to persuade Captain Miller is the fact that Miller is an intellectual himself (he's a teacher, he quotes Emerson). He is unlike Upham only in that he has by force of brute will obliged all cowardice from his own body except for his symptomatically quaking right hand. This hand, foregrounded by Spielberg again and again, is synecdoche for the general cowardice of intellectuals. But Miller is bravely determined that he will not allow cowardice to dominate himself in particular.

Of course all this is called into question later. Matters are complicated at the film's climax when (and here is Spielberg's *deus ex machina* at its extreme) this same German prisoner returns to shoot and kill our heroic Captain Miller. The German peers in satisfaction. It was a good shot. Fuck that American *schweinhund*. Him and Betty Boop. Meanwhile, the cowardly intellectual Upham cringes in a crater, hugging his feckless rifle as if it were a favorite and comforting doll. The contempt we feel for him. Our self-disgust at once having sympathized with his intellectualization, his reasons. Our national sorrow that the great man, Captain Miller, must die as a consequence of Upham's lack of manliness. We'll never make *that* mistake again. We'll go with what our gut tells us.

The Great Change. Immediately following Miller's death, Upham experiences a great change. It is as if Miller's courage has flowed over to Upham at the moment of his death. The son Upham becomes the father Captain Miller. Upham leaps from his hiding place in the crater—all nervousness gone, rifle at the ready, the very image of resoluteness, of hard experience. He improbably persuades six or seven Germans to drop their weapons (instead of shooting the hell out of him). One of these soldiers is, of course, our German prisoner, the guy upon whom Upham had wasted his powers of compassion and ethical reasoning. Hopeful that again his naive advocate would aid him, the

German gestures hands forward and says, "Upham!" Buddy! At which point Upham murders him. In the logic of the film, he does what should have been done the first time.

Do I need to say this? The second meeting between Upham and the German is not ironic. It is contrived. Spielberg is insisting on our attention to this point. We will not be allowed to miss his meaning. And a brutal meaning it is. Emotionally, it is clear that Spielberg anticipates that the audience's response to Upham's act will be full-throttle approval. "Yeah! At last! Revenge is sweet! Just what the treacherous Kraut deserved." (I really never imagined that I would ever again be given license to hate Germans. But for the length of this movie, at least, they are again Krauts. Their appeals to their common or shared humanity are all duplicity and self-interest. They are what they are: Nazis. Krauts. If death is theirs, it's fitting.) Thus the film's murderous thesis is fully disclosed. Self-survival, the survival of the good, requires that one choose death. The cynicism and brutality of the first executions back on Omaha Beach are excused in their fact if not in their style. Bad table manners, perhaps, but in murdering the prisoners the American soldiers did what they had to do. This is advocacy of international vigilantism and no whit more self-reflective than any Dirty Harry narrative.

It's the sort of moral imperative that *ought* (and how contrary is this *ought!*) to make us understand why those on the wrong side of our national self-righteousness and cruise missiles ("pharmaceuticists" in the Sudan and other Muslim countries, for example) have this imponderable desire to blow up our embassies. Could it be because they understand (as well they should!) our national logic better than we do? Aren't they saying to us, "You know, it's easy to choose death for other people. Let us show you how it feels to have death chosen for you. Arbitrarily. A bolt from the clear blue."

Closing. With the words of Abraham Lincoln echoing in the background (pride, sacrifice, glory, freedom—it's 1915 again and we're all dying sweetly *pro patria!*), the weepy vet returns to the screen. We know now that the man is Ryan. And the question he asks (a question that is really a narrative *non sequitur*, given the film's foregrounding of the Upham story) is: "Have I lived a good life? Have I been a good man?"

Well, with his granddaughters' lovely bosoms still hanging like a majestic sunset in the background, how can we say anything but yes?

Or, more reasonably, well, how the hell are we supposed to know if the poor son of a bitch led a good life? His wife doesn't look beat up. But that nose! How much gin did you knock back, Papa? How much TV did you watch? How many peaceniks did you rail against during Vietnam? How many Nazis did you help elect to Congress, with your little democratic ballot, so like a bullet to the rest of the world? What do you think of Rush Limbaugh and Newt Gingrich? Do you hate the eggheads as much as Spielberg seems to think you should? How many times did you curse the EPA because it got in the way of some concrete you wanted to pour?

Sorry if these questions are inappropriate, but you don't fool me. I remember those VFW papas well. I remember their malice for the Japs and Krauts. The gooks and the slants. I'm patient. I can wait for your responses to my questions. But till you have them, you'll excuse me if I don't join this orgy of nationalist *amour propre* uniting VFW dads and their contrite sons. (Hasn't *that* been a sight at the local cineplex!) We should all know too well what such self-love is a preparation for.

4.

In the thoroughly managed and self-surveilling world of the Middle Mind, how, we ought to ask, is it ever possible to create real art? How does anyone manage to elude its charming devices? Or how, as the great social theorist Theodor Adorno put it, can an autonomous or free art be produced in a context of enduring societal unfreedom? Spielberg's films are not "free." They unroll under heavy ideological and aesthetic obligations (even if Spielberg is perfectly happy to acknowledge and live by these obligations). The question before us is how others might elude Spielberg's fate. Adorno's ideas on art can help.

Adorno's notorious Dialectic of Enlightenment consists substantially of the movement between the universal and the particular. In art, the universal is the law of genre, a "collective bindingness." And so, for example, if Mr. Spielberg is to make a war movie, he feels bound by the law of genre to have rippling flags, heroes, and gut-wrenching spasms of patriotism. On the other side, the particular (or the individual and subjective) represents the theoretically boundless world of human possibility and play (which Adorno attempts to capture through the word *spontaneity*). The flag and so much more in *Saving Private Ryan* are not playful or spontaneous; they are abject. They are bent beneath the burden of what is expected and tolerated (even if richly rewarded).

Art is most itself, is "true" art, when it makes itself not through the conventions of the universal (genre: the rules for the proper construction of sonata or sonnet, or, as with *Saving Private Ryan*, the rote fulfillment of generic expectation) but, as Adorno thought, "by virtue of its own elaborations, through its own immanent process." (205) Laurence Sterne understood this in the eighteenth century as the only true law of the novel: the novel is the "art of digression." To be sure, these elaborations can deploy themselves only in a context made available by historical conventions; nonetheless, when an artwork is successful, it is in spite of the presence of convention and not because of it. This is why, ultimately, craft has little to do with whether or not a work is a successful piece of art.

The most powerful and sinister gambit of what Adorno calls "administered society" is to promise the freedom of individuality while simultaneously prohibiting it. For example, consumers have been promised the "freedom of the open road" by auto-makers for the last half-century, but with each passing year the realization of that freedom becomes more unlikely for all the familiar reasons (not least of which is the perverse insistence of other individuals to use the same roads promised for *your* freedom). Or, more to our point, the Middle Mind offers us an art and a cultural commentary that is really just more commercial product. The promise of art becomes its betrayal.

Art is a response to this repression. The exemplary works of artistic autonomy were, for Adorno, the "experimental" works of modernism, especially the music of Arnold Schoenberg and the anti-novels of Samuel Beckett. For us, however, the failure of—or, we might say, the passing of—the opportunity for modernism leaves us in a situation that can still be thought through in Adorno's terms but not with his examples.

The one area in contemporary culture in which the administered universal and the particular (with its impulse to freedom) continue a consequential and sometimes deadly engagement is in the theater provided by "rock." In an otherwise domesticated art world, rock still has the potential for what Adorno called "social explosiveness." This is not news that he would have been happy to hear. For Adorno, the idea that the struggle for the virtue of "spontaneity" was being waged within pop culture would have been the assurance of its failure.

I wouldn't contend otherwise. I would contend only that the Music Industry, this profitable and well-managed sector of the Culture Industry, is also the place where the question of authenticity (understood as the freedom to wander from convention) is most broadly and dramatically engaged. It is here, and not in the experimental novel or in poetry, that artists can still have broad social consequence, as the Beatles, the Grateful Dead, the Sex Pistols, and now perhaps Radiohead can testify. But the fact that the dialectic of the universal and particular, the Dialectic of Enlightenment, is still forcefully and fatefully alive in popular music does not mean that it is not also doomed, and well in advance. For rock music, too, must seize its possibility in the context of its impossibility.

Consider the instance of Radiohead and its controversial album *Kid A*. The music of *Kid A* and its public reception made explicit the drama implicit in the relationship between an autonomous art (or, at

least, an art with the desire for autonomy) and an administered culture. Take, for example, the review of *Kid A* written by novelist Nick
Hornby ("Beyond the Pale," the *New Yorker*, October 30, 2000).

Hornby's review is not an objective evaluation of an artwork. It is
the reassertion of a familiar, grim, and very repressive aesthetic.
Hornby begins his review with the obligatory homage to Ray Charles
and Elvis Presley, thus establishing his orthodoxy, his faithfulness to
the one true Church of the Commodified Vernacular. Hornby can
then begin to lay out the aesthetic grounds for Radiohead's heresy to
what Hornby calls "the old-fashioned dynamics of rock": *Kid A* demands the patience of the devoted; both patience and devotion become scarcer commodities once you start picking up a paycheck.

Could he be any plainer? Art is about exchange. We give the artist
our hard-earned money and the artist . . . what? Doesn't try our patience?

Hornby gives more content to what it is we expect in return for
that which we've given from our paycheck. Hornby argues that Radiohead's previous album, *OK Computer*, had "some extraordinarily
lovely tracks," and in *Kid A*'s best moments "something gorgeous floats
past." So, in the World of Art according to Nick Hornby, the first and
highest principle is that it should be a fair exchange—you should "get
your money's worth" (as his mother probably told him)—and aesthetic
tenet number two is that the art should be "gorgeous" and also maybe
a little bit "lovely." Now, beyond the obvious fact that this is an old romantic tautology and Hornby has no idea what he's talking about, it
does reveal that the fundamental premise of Hornby's aesthetic insistence is pleasure. My money is well spent if I "enjoy" the album/movie/
sitcom/football game.

As Adorno put it, pithily, "Whoever concretely enjoys artworks is a
philistine; he is convicted by expressions like 'a feast for the ears.'" (13)
Hornby's aesthetic is the aesthetic of the balance sheet: "Heard the
Ninth Symphony last night, enjoyed myself so and so much." (13) As
Adorno concludes, and Hornby substantiates, "such feeble-mindedness
has by now established itself as common sense." (13)

Not to cheat Hornby of the full import of his thought (feeble-mindedness notwithstanding), he also suggests that it is good for art to have a message. "*Pablo Honey* [Radiohead's first album] . . . contained one song, 'Creep,' that gave voice to everyone who has ever felt disconnected, alienated, or geeky. . . ." So, in summary, art should be a fair exchange of money for pleasure, and it's nice if it also can "give voice" to something—a message, or something that someone somewhere once "felt."

To be sure, there is also *ad hominem* innuendo, in case the reasoning behind this hatchet job is too subtle for you, reader of the esteemed *New Yorker*. Radiohead is a "band that has come to hate itself"; it has suffered a "failure of courage"; and, that old kumquat served to the experimental, the band has been "self-indulgent" in making its music.

Well, I can't defend Radiohead from these charges because, to tell you the truth, I've never met the guys and as far as I know they might hate themselves, they might indeed lack courage, and they might be self-indulgent as all get out. Hey, some folks are. But I do have an alternative hypothesis, one that strikes me as being very probable indeed: this is a band that hates *you*, Nick Hornby, you and your ilk, with your philistine taste and the abominable arrogance which allows you to claim you know what rock 'n' roll ought to be about. Rock 'n' roll is about "fair exchange of money for pleasure"?! You are the very Soul Man, aren't you?

The real basis of Hornby's critique is this: Radiohead is perverse. Hornby imagines his ideal art consumer yelling at *Kid A*, "You're supposed to be a pop group! . . . You're supposed to use your gifts for songwriting, and singing, and playing."

You're supposed to be a commodity, stupid! Just make your money and give us what we expect.

But of course Radiohead has made it loudly and widely known that it did not set out to be a commodity; it set out to make art, which is to say that no band since Nirvana has made it more abundantly clear that its "intention" (for what that's worth) is to seize freedom from the context of unfreedom.[7] As I've argued, only the popular music scene allows for this as a possibility on such an international stage, but the crazy-making irony is that this intent cannot be realized in the only context in which it is possible even to express the intent.

"Fuck Corporate Rock!"

"Can we put that on a T-shirt and sell it at the concert?"

"Yeah, sure, man. What's our cut?"

Commodify your dissent. Ask Kurt Cobain about how it works in practice.

Fortunately, Radiohead is politically savvy in a way that Cobain rarely was. (The fact that the band members were serious music students and not heroin addicts probably didn't hurt.) Radiohead's political *bête noir* is what Adorno called "instrumental rationality." A techno-totalized world. Its artistic quandary is not how to prosper within this totalized context (as their well-wisher Nick Hornby encourages), but how to respond to it in a way that is adequate to what the artist wants: the feel of the authentic, the spontaneity of autonomy, even a tiny gap between itself and the universal other, the Corporate Life World.

Call it a self-indulgent refusal of their job description (why, "there's no room for anything approaching conventional pop music," Hornby whines), but this is the obligation or the duty, if you will, that art itself feels it owes to the social. It's as if art's primary function were simply to remind us that there is a difference between freedom and repression. It reminds us that change is real and the possible is possible. Art's job is to give us objects that argue forcefully that there is a difference between feeling alive and feeling dead.

The problem, though, is that a strategy to create this gap between itself and the world of dead convention works for a period but is then used up ("entombed in the pantheon of cultural commodities," [228] as Adorno put it) and a new strategy must be discovered. At times,

---

[7] I could add the alt-groups Sonic Youth, the Flaming Lips, the Breeders, the Mekons, or Wilco to this list. Rather than carping about my choices, readers should feel free to supply their own favorite alt-cult rock-hero list at this point.

Kid A seems like a catalogue of devices that have been used to create this gap between the artwork and the law of the universal:

- dissonant orchestral waves (in the cut "How to Disappear Completely")

- avant-garde free jazz extrapolations à la Mingus ("National Anthem")

- surreal lyrics and aural landscapes ("Threefingers")

- punk/grunge crudeness in bass lines and guitar crunching ("National Anthem")

- homage to Beatles avant-gardism in the echoes of Ringo's drum rhythms on "Strawberry Fields Forever" ("Kid A")

- electronic ambience à la Brian Eno ("Motion Picture Soundtrack")

- psychedelic noodling in guitar lines ("In Limbo")

- homages to Led Zep vocal and guitar breakthroughs—what Jeff Beck called the sound of "my guitar being sick" ("In Limbo")

- sampling and a general feel of the aesthetics of pastiche (rooting the band not only in hip-hop but also in Dada) ("Idioteque")

In the most expansive and forceful cuts on this album—"National Anthem" and "Idioteque"—it seems as if nearly *all* of these strategies are brought to the fore. But no one of these strategies is sufficient for Radiohead's ultimate purposes. It's as if they wanted to provide a historical reprise of oppositional strategies before coming to their own most central concerns.

In short, as its name, the titles of its last two albums, most of its lyrics, and all of the graphics clearly indicate, Radiohead is centrally concerned with the following questions: What does it mean to be a human being in a context in which every relationship is mediated by technology and technical rationality? (How can we "live and breathe" when "everyone is broken," they ask in *The Bends*, explicitly if unintentionally echoing the ethical thinking behind Adorno's concept of "damage.") And Radiohead asks, What does it mean to be artists opposed to technical rationality when we are obliged not only to create our art through computers, in highly technical and utterly engineered recording studios, but also in cooperation with international mega-corporations? (These boys are not Ani DiFranco with her own publishing, recording, and distribution setup; these boys are with EMI/Capitol.) For the most prominent stylistic force on *Kid A* is techno. Synthetic sound, synthetic rhythm. And what is most plaintive and appealing in Radiohead's art are the moments in which it contrives to allow its own voice, its created "style," its humanity in an utterly nineteenth-century sense, to transcend, to rise above the unfreedom of their context and even the conventionalized unfreedom of their own medium, pop music. In these inspired moments of Mahlerian sweetness, the band rises above the shit of our shared condition. (What else does Mahler try to do, in symphony after symphony, but dramatize this one desire?) In a cut called "Exit Music" on *OK Computer*, the angelic but synthetic background chorus makes it seem as if Radiohead wished to inspire even the androids to claim humanity. And there is a weird pathos in the computer-processed speaking voice on "Fitter Happier" and the lead vocal on "Kid A," a song that could be called "The Robot Child's Lament."

Radiohead's aesthetic strategy is not to avoid the enemy but to inhabit it and reorient its energies. As Buddhists would argue, there is nothing inherently evil about machines; even computers are okay. It's the mind that inhabits the machine that can be malign. What really bugs critics like Nick Hornby is that as Radiohead's albums have progressed, this strategy has not been taken up through an explicit "message" in the lyrics while the music remains more-or-less standard pop-rock (even if very good pop-rock). Rather, the group's thinking has been taken up more integrally in the textures of the music itself. This is what sends *Kid A* "beyond the pale." In fact, I would argue that Radiohead's intuition that their politics are best made not explicitly in their lyrics but integrally with the music is a very good indication of the artistic and political health of the band. By so doing, they not only elude Hornby's commodity fetishism but they also refuse the error of politically correct art, which seeks to make its artistic effect dependent on the virtue of its political message. As Adorno writes,

> Artworks that want to divest themselves of fetishism by real and extremely dubious political commitment regularly enmesh themselves in false consciousness as the result of inevitable and vainly praised simplification. In the shortsighted praxis to which they blindly subscribe, their own blindness is prolonged. (228)

Don't misunderstand me. Radiohead's *Kid A* is "dead" more often than it is alive. (Or as Theodore Roszak put it thirty-plus years ago in *The Making of a Counter Culture*, "[T]he counterculture arrives, not trailing clouds of glory, but bearing the mark of the beast." (73)) Radiohead is a pop band. Its music is finally "acceptable." The harmonic structure of its music is more often conventional than not. How else could it be second, in *USA Today*'s 2001 best-of-the-year evaluation, only to U2 (those other artist-critics of the same Culture Industry that made them rich and famous)? But anything that escapes the great maw of the universal is *ipso facto* subversive and dangerous. And so enough light escapes to allow us to imagine that perhaps they're not entirely dead, and so perhaps we're not entirely dead, and so perhaps something other than the smothering present is *possible*.

With admirable frequency, Radiohead's music realizes this enormous purpose, to achieve the human in the midst of the inhuman, the free in the midst of the unfree. In an instant. With all the unexpected grace of a little amber light discovered above a sick man's hospital bed. The wonderfulness of that instant is all we have any right to ask for. As Radiohead says on "Exit Music": "Breathe. Keep breathing."

One of the great tragedies in public discourse in the United States is that what we need most (powerful intelligence) we forbid. This happens through shallow assumptions about genre (philosophy and pop culture don't belong together: pop is for us, philosophy is for academics); a centuries-old disdain for intellectuals (often thoroughly deserved, I might add, and if you have any questions about why, you need do no more than consult Rabelais's satire of scholasticists in *Gargantua and Pantagruel*); and the rigidity of the mass media itself, its impermeability to thought. In discussing Radiohead in the context of the thought of Theodor Adorno, I have performed an unnatural act (as Lenny Bruce once called sex between the Lone Ranger and Tonto [or Tonto *and* Silver!]). I have asked you to imagine that the thought of Theodor Adorno, abstruse German philosopher, is useful in thinking about what the British pop band Radiohead represents. I have even asked you to imagine that Adorno is important to our happiness in the most ordinary sense. My interest in the imagination *is* an interest in the possibility of happiness. As William Carlos Williams wrote of the imagination's promise:

> So most of my life has been lived in hell—a hell of repression
> lit by flashes of inspiration, when a poem such as this or that
> would appear
>   What would have happened in a world similarly lit by the
> imagination (116)

This "hell of repression" that Williams speaks of is made possible and maintained by certain mass delusions. Like the delusion that the Entertainment State is good for us, is entertaining, is a hoot, the kids love it, when is that damned new *Star Wars* episode coming out? I can't stand the excitement waiting for the next installment of our national "classic," where ham-handed acting and plotting equals art. Through the ministrations of the Middle Mind, entertainment is art, a conclusion we seem deliriously happy with from the top to the bottom of our culture. What we don't acknowledge, to our misery, is that because of this confusion, this inability to keep the distinction between art and its others cogent, we have nearly no art at all.

Chapter 2

SUCH AN AWESOME SITE
OF RESISTANCE

I don't know what to say about American Cultural Studies.
I am completely dumbfounded by it.
Stuart Hall

1.

What I have been trying to establish is the idea that the poverty of the imagination is first a poverty of reading. Criticism creates the opportunity for creativity. We are poor because we cannot read and reconstruct even the crude ideological narratives of the media, and, as my old teacher Merle Brown tried to show, we are poor because we are no longer sufficiently interested in what a poem does to provide the *care* that should go into reading it, allowing it to perform itself with our participation and cooperation as readers. As Brown saw, the devolution of reading and criticism was inaugurated by deconstruction even if that was in no way deconstruction's philosophic purpose. It has been sad to witness the devolution of reading in universities, because when I was a student I assumed that the university was about the only place where that sort of care and attention to literature and art still mattered. So egregious has this lack of care become in some quarters that the refusal to read has become a reluctance even to *look*.

In a case that is emblematic in my mind, in 1994 at Illinois State University, the University Gallery brought in an exhibition of paintings by Mike Cockrill. The paintings depicted adolescent and pre-adolescent girls in a variety of precociously sexual poses. A scandal erupted around these paintings, with opponents accusing the university of supporting child pornography. But none of the exhibition's critics seemed interested in reading the paintings. They were interested only in locating the artist's (vile) political "position." Everyone in the community was talking about the paintings, but no one was looking at them with much care. We had been humiliated by a political critique into a shamed averting of our eyes from exactly that which was meant to be the focus of our attention. "Will you 'gaze' upon the paintings?" became a kind of political litmus test that precluded all other discussion. But when I took the risky step of daring to read the paintings, it became clear to me that the exhibition was exactly about libido and complicity. What gives us pleasure is corrupt, just as art's own powerful seductions are often not pure but corrupted by the ills of the social moment. Cockrill's paintings mixed equal parts of horror and indulgence. The paintings neither bluntly blamed (as anti-porn advocates might like) nor entirely volupted (as pornographers might like). The paintings created emotional, libidinal, and political instabilities. These instabilities are mirrored in the paintings' formal strategies, which move between commercial, pornographic, and Beaux Arts technical conventions. A thrilling opportunity to read had been passed over for the sake of the virtuous feeling of political certainty.

This devolution of reading in the academy is largely the consequence of the ascendancy of Cultural Studies in North American universities. In the messy instability following New Criticism's demise, it was Cultural Studies that emerged as the new dominant, the new stamp in which all Ph.D.s would be minted. In the hands of its original thinkers—Stuart Hall and Raymond Williams in particular, in their famous Birmingham Center for Contemporary Cultural Studies—Cultural Studies was a lucid and necessary examination of the relationship of culture (whether high culture or working-class culture) to the administrative state. The most important, fundamental, and incontestable claim of early Cultural Studies was the simple idea that culture was political. However, in universities in the United States in the 1980s and '90s, Cultural Studies experienced an explosive growth leading to a curious institutionalization and professionalization of what had begun as a marginal and Marx-inspired movement. American Cultural Studies was driven by three primary methods, most of which would have surprised the Birmingham founders: semiotics (the language of "social construction," of culture as a vast "text"); feminism, race studies, and Queer Theory (which together constituted the "politics of difference" and "identity politics" and effectively excluded Cultural Studies' original concern, the broader tradition of "class"); and the celebration of commercially developed "popular" culture (the very commercial culture that had been the enemy of working-class culture for the earliest cultural theorists). These three tendencies in North American universities were the advance guard for the left in the so-called Culture Wars of the eighties and nineties. Beyond infuriating the right, which it certainly did, Cultural Studies had very damaging, if less visible, consequences for literature, which was swamped by undifferentiated "signifying practices," PC guilt, and Bart Simpson dolls.

The reading of literary texts in the humanities dominated by Cultural Studies has become a matter of searching the text for symptoms supporting the sociopolitical or theoretical template of the critic. The political/theoretical template (whether provided by Louis Althusser, Homi Bhabha, Antonio Gramsci, Donna Haraway, or a host of others) comes first, and what's in the poem or essay or novel is determined by the template. As art critic Libby Lumpkin argues in her book *Deep Design* (1999),

> So deeply are [present-day academicians] invested in the construction of art as philosophy that they have dispensed with the bulk of the language once used to describe material objects. Despite the fact that art must, by definition, embody its meaning, the term "form" is censored or disparaged.[1] (112)

---

[1] Worse yet, this political/critical tendency has affected the thinking of artists themselves. As Julie Caniglia put it in her essay "57 Cultures and Nothing On" (*Minneapolis City Pages*, April 24, 1996), "The multiculturalism that appeared so revolutionary 10 years ago has curdled into a fractious politics of identity, resulting in a new and, for the most part, incredibly banal didacticism: work that 'explores' this personal issue or 'documents' that social problem, that 'provokes' the viewer regarding the artist's identity, or 'confronts' the artist's traumas (usually of childhood origins). . . . As

Cultural Studies' "reading after symptoms" has had a flattening effect on literature, because all texts can be said to contain "signifiers" acting as "social symptoms." Consequently, the literary text becomes one "signifying practice" among many. Literature becomes just another "discursive formation." A TV commercial, a sitcom, a tabloid treatment of OJ, a poem by Yeats—they're all "manifestations of culture." This tends to flatten culture, abolish distinction, make everything gray, just as much as *Fresh Air*'s juxtaposition-without-comment (as if it were the most natural and even perspicuous thing in the world) of Christoph Eschenbach and Barry Manilow tends to flatten. In academia, Cultural Studies has done much the same thing with Milton and Madonna, as conservative critics like George Will remind us *ad nauseam*. The problem here isn't that this juxtaposition violates old high/low distinctions. The problem is that this kind of reading destroys *all* difference. It impoverishes. It creates Hegel's "night in which all cows are black." Even though the academy has a hard time acknowledging this complicity with the Middle Mind's tendency to flatten, it is obvious even to mainstream writers like John Seabrook, distinguished Nobrowologist, a person not always willing to acknowledge what he sees, as I have already noted. Seabrook writes that his introduction to Nobrow was not on Madison Avenue; it was in Raymond Williams's Cultural Studies seminar at Oxford in 1983. "The Williams seminar now seems like the real beginning of my education in Nobrow—the real world of culture that I was working in at Tina Brown's *New Yorker*." (53) At Oxford, the party line was that aesthetics was all politics; it was all about the ideology of "taste" and "class hegemony," short and sweet. This line hasn't changed much since then.

The fundamental lack in the approach taken by American Cultural Studies is that it looks at culture only as a critic, as a member of the faith of criticism, and it can't imagine what it might mean to look

---

[1] (continued) art gets parsed into a multitude of niches based on identity, it follows that the standards for judging such work are lowered, eliminated, or qualified into irrelevance."

at texts from the perspective of artists. (For good or bad, this was not a problem that the leading New Critics had, many of whom, like John Crowe Ransom, were also practicing poets.) For an artist, difference is everything. The difference between the hack, the dilettante, and the artist as both master of a tradition and inventor of the "best next thing" (as one of our greatest literary artists, John Barth, put it) is everything. The reason that these distinctions are important has nothing to do with supporting high culture, or disdaining pop culture, or maintaining standards, or appealing to timeless and transcendental notions of the beautiful. It is much simpler than that. It has to do with the difference between feeling alive and feeling dead. For an artist to make something that is mere conventional hackwork is to feel dead in a way that is fundamentally defeating. On the other hand, to make something that has the click of invention (the "autonomy" that Adorno refers to) is to feel that life has been pulled from the abyss called death of perception wherein one is dumbly pent by Stevens's quotidian or Hegel's "night," the night of the Middle Mind dead. Each day's practice is the requirement of going once more to that abyss, where life's failure is a real possibility, and plucking life out in the possibility (if not the realization) of its human capacity. This cannot be done in a context in which, as Stevens wrote, "the deer and the dachshund" (or Eschenbach and Manilow) are one. It can be done only in a world in which the imagination rules supreme and, as Stevens writes again, "the rabbit is the king of ghosts." Thus, art's ongoing power, whether in Beethoven, Coltrane, or Radiohead, is that this call to life is powerful and intuitively persuasive (as old Plato knew, which is why he banished it from his ideal republic). Art is always necessarily a threat to the Reign of the Dictatorship of the Present.

And so when Cultural Studies race theorist Cornel West, good and smart man though he is, argues in "The New Cultural Politics of Difference" (his contribution to *The Cultural Studies Reader*) that the politics of difference ought to inform the work of the artist of the future, the artist in me winces. West argues that artists should think of themselves as "culture workers" and should "align themselves with demoralized, demobilized, depoliticized, and disorganized people in order to empower and enable social action." (257) This, surely, is a vision of the artist that is virtuous as all get out, but it is also a recipe for bad art. Probably a lot of bad art. Hung on the walls of coffee shops and hung on the walls of the local museum, sponsored by a corporate foundation in need of the appearance of social conscience; spouted from the lips of distinguished visiting writers and spouted from open mike poetry readings *ad nauseam*. And so I have to say that I don't think Cornel West knows what he's talking about. He advocates art as social activism. I don't think West understands how art functions and how it has its social impact. Art is not the display of self-congratulatory social virtue. Period. And no amount of complaining by social activist artists about the unfairness of having to prove themselves "in light of norms and models set by white elites whose own heritage devalued and dehumanized them" will make bad art good. For an artist, West's recommendation that artists think of themselves as "Critical Organic Catalysts" (265) must sound bizarre and frightening. Worse yet, it sounds deadening.

Stevens again:

> In this area of my subject I might be expected to speak of the social, that is to say sociological or political, obligation of the poet. He has none. . . . No politician can command the imagination, directing it to do this or that. Stalin might grind his teeth the whole of a Russian winter and yet all the poets in the Soviets might remain silent the following spring. (27–28)

Cultural Studies is also dead to something any artist must be sensitive to: how the past lingers for an artist. Cultural Studies' interest in time has to do with paradigm shifts and radical breaks. The biggest "scoop" in this intellectual world is to be the first to identify and name the current "moment." Everyone wants to be the next Jean-François Lyotard writing *The Postmodern Condition*. "Until further notice, you are to think of yourselves as living in postmodernity. No, make that late capitalism. Wait, it's really the postcolonial moment. Hold it, the post-human. I'll have to get back to you on this." Believe me, reputations are made, contracts are signed, product is distributed, conferences are proposed in sunny places like UCLA and Duke, or not so sunny places like New Haven. This is the best academic buzz there is: to announce that the present is dead and long live the present. That gets you the "go straight to Yale" card. Once we've gone on to the next stage, all the rules change, and appeals to past organizations are by mysterious edict ruled out of order. There is an absolutism in Cultural Studies' understanding of time.

Cultural Studies utterly fails to see why certain aspects of the past are values that we ought to want to insist on. This is something that artists understand very concretely. The past is something that lingers. It is carried in the body. The internalized music of Shakespeare's phrasing, that is what matters to the artist, not his status as Harold Bloom's culture hero. That odd bloody brown in Rembrandt. These qualities of the past become visceral for artists, and it is through their present works that the *body* of the past stays alive for us. An artist worthy of the name is like the pianist who studied with a master who studied with Bartók who studied with István Thomán who studied with Liszt, and so it is not too much to say that that attack on that phrase, that feel, that quality of technical care, is old Liszt himself talking to us. It's like in Buddhism, where the assumption is that every *rinpoche* studied in a tradition and a lineage that began with the Buddha himself. And every member of the community gains a feeling of connectedness to a human past of great value through this *rinpoche*. This is so even as we move forward to invent the Buddha of the Future.

Where is Cultural Studies' concern for this sort of experience of human time? What we fail to see in Cultural Studies' putative left radicalism is just how *rationalist*, how abstract and "disembodied" its jargon is. In the corporate university of the (very near) future, Cultural Studies will find a welcome place provided for it. It has done international capitalism the favor of dismantling the disciplinary structure of the old bourgeois university; it has made reading a matter of technical competence in "discursive formations" and "signifying practices" across fields; it has rationalized and abstracted the traditional work of the arts and humanities, devaluing and dismissing them as the products of "elites"; it has given itself over to technical professionalization; it has aided and abetted in the flattening of differences in the culture as a whole; it has worked in such a way that its creations are inseparable from the marketing of popular culture in the mass media (how many Peewee Herman dolls? how many *Star Wars* action figures? how many Madonna albums? how many *Simpsons* videos? how many semiotically turned episodes of *General Hospital?*); and all of this it has done in the name of a *left* critique! For capitalism, who needs friends like Reagan education and drug czar William Bennett when you have enemies like these? Constance Penley, professor of film studies, writes, "It is probably obvious to you from my tone here that I am, for the most part, completely gaga over . . . [*Star Trek*] fandom. It indeed represents the most radical and intriguing female appropriation of a mass-produced cultural product that I have ever seen. A friend of mine told me that I wasn't really a fan of *Star Trek*, I was a fan of this fandom, and I think there is a great deal of truth in that." (491) But what I would like to know is what difference this distinction makes. I don't discount the idea that women can take *Star Trek* and appropriate it for their own lively purposes, and I say more power to them. What I question is Penley's interest in their activities. Is she a participant? No, she's a postmodern ethnologist visiting a subculture. What she does clearly do is promote a general interest in *Star Trek* that those interested in marketing its products can have little problem with. Sounds like a lot of product-licensing opportunities to them.[2]

As for the grating sounds that the Professors of Signs make when referring to Marx, or Queers, or feminism, who cares? These sounds are entirely managed (literally, *institutionalized*) by academic culture,

---

[2] As of November 1, 2002, Accoutrements, a wholesale company that describes itself as "Outfitters of Popular Culture," had sold 10,884 Sigmund Freud action figures, according to their Web site.

and they have next to no practical effects outside of that context. Talk about "false consciousness"!

The huge irony here is that what cultural conservatives like George Will fear most, that the values of a shared cultural tradition are being lost, has come true. But traditional culture has not been lost to the efforts of academic leftists. It has been lost to Will's own beloved free market economy moving ever further into its international mode. It is capitalism that looks without pity on Will's cultural sentimentality. What does Shakespeare matter to George Bush II? Hey, George Will, Bush doesn't even like your precious Cubs! Wrigley Field? Fuck it! Sell it to the Japanese and build something in its place with lots of luxury boxes where corporate execs can munch sushi and watch Sosa launch homers. If nobody but Stupid White Men (in Michael Moore's endearing phrase) can afford to go to the game, who cares?

On the other side, the joy of Cultural Studies in its conquest of the humanities in academic America must come tempered by the understanding that it is not its leftism that allows it to win, but its unacknowledged complicity with the globalized corporate culture of the future.

My criticism of Cultural Studies is as much concerned with how it has been institutionalized, taken up into the daily practices of the *Lumpenprofessoriat*, as it is with specific canonical texts of Cultural Studies. How has the influence of Cultural Studies been lived in classrooms, seminars, dissertations, job presentations, and conferences? As Lisa Ruddick of the University of Chicago writes in the November 23, 2001, issue of the *Chronicle of Higher Education*,

> After I finished my first book 11 years ago and was suddenly freed by tenure from the necessity of adhering to the critical norms of the moment, I became, disappointingly, paralyzed. I was in great conflict about continuing to observe certain intellectual rules that were a part of the dominant thinking—rules that I thought were very limiting but that I couldn't challenge without courting disgrace. . . .

I remember a particularly bad season when I struggled with an article on *Ulysses*. I was writing about Joyce's insights into the touching human need to bury, burn, or otherwise take care of the bodies of the dead—an impulse that is universal. . . . Yet I was still afraid I'd be attacked for "essentializing"—for supposing that there are shared features that constitute the essence of being human.

Cultural studies has radically remade the professionalization of the study of literature, creating a new conformism in the process. Worse yet, it has undercut its own political premises of "political engagement." The brawny lingo of "intervention" and "interrogation" are now not much more than respectful professional markers that cause no one anxiety, not in the dean's office, not in the mayor's office, not in the state legislature, not with the local congressional representative, and certainly not in the offices of CEOs and branch managers who now count on the technically literate and conceptually sophisticated graduates of these programs for the next generation of entry-level employees for USA.com. It doesn't even create anxiety in English departments any longer, because most of the students of the New Critical period have gone off into that sweet good night of the academic pension. No. Cultural Studies is now safely institutionalized in the contemporary university of "excellence," where administrators can refer to it as a "best practice" in reading.

Cultural Studies has always lived in danger of being seduced by its object, especially when that object was commercial popular culture (that great unresolved oxymoron) or, more recently, technology. Just at the moment that its critical gaze is set to reveal the Entertainment State or techno-rationalism, an intravenous drip-line is inserted directly into some subtle pleasure center in the critic. (It's a part of the brain that's shaped like Mr. Spock in silhouette.) Or perhaps the right metaphor is that the culture, like a sea urchin, has inserted its stomach into the critic and is dissolving her from the inside. "Cultural Studies demonstrates the social difference that theory can make," says the brave critic. But now the aggressive edge of the critic softens as the urchin stomach does its work. Now the critic looks a little doe-eyed. Now she's mumbling something about how cool virtual reality is. How American popular culture rocks. Finally, the critic asks for the little cute ET doll to cuddle with and sighs, "This is such an awesome site of resistance."

Cultural Studies needs a good theme song, and I suggest Radiohead's cunning "You and Whose Army," in which the Holy Roman Empire is challenged to "come out if you think you can take us all." Meanwhile, it sounds very much as if we're all falling asleep or into a very deep and incontestable languor.

2.

I want to pursue a little further the effect of the growth of Cultural Studies in academia, especially in the context of the Culture Wars, and above all in that battleground referred to as the Western Canon, a battleground that Cultural Studies' taste for identity politics and pop culture has claimed as its own. I think that what has happened in these so-called Culture Wars has been unfortunate, unnecessary, and destructive of the social and artistic health of the imagination. A review of the positions of the academic left and conservative traditionalists should reveal that the Culture Wars are a mere sideshow in relationship to the real action: the operations of the media-oriented Middle Mind. Taking sides in this pitched battle royal, the Great Canon Debate, the most recent Battle of the Books in which moderns fight it out with classics, is a fruitless diversion. Commitment to either side is an error, especially as the Middle Mind marches on, its truth on four hundred clear channels, coming soon in HDTV, wireless, broadbanded, and downloadable into every frontal lobe. (Just when we thought lobotomies were a thing of the past!) Neither side offers opportunity to the imagination. The academic left's relentless rhetoric of "resistance" is couched in purely sociological terms that exclude the importance of the aesthetic. The traditional practices of the humanities, based in deep engagement with primary artistic texts and not abstract theoretical renderings, provided clear instances of art's capacity for creating imaginative environments. Cut off from such an understanding of its history, the imagination dries up. On the other hand, the traditionalist's call to our cultural legacy as a simple catalogue of perfections without contexts, distant and arid museum pieces, denies to the imagination any sense of how those earlier works might inform the work of the present. In any event, both tendencies are impoverishing, and it's worth our while to see just how that's so.

Ground Zero for the Culture Wars has been the so-called literary *canon*, a term originally used in order to account for what books are and what books are not part of the Bible. The Torah, or Pentateuch, is a canon. It is those five books and no others that make up the Old Testament. *Canon* is, without question, a loaded and probably very wrong concept to use in order to talk about literary or artistic works. (When exactly did we accept the idea that art needed a bible?) If we must, however, use this term, I think it behooves us to use it knowingly. The root of the word *canon* does not mean "those things which are properly included." The root word (from the Greek, *kanon*) means a device for *measuring* what ought to go in whatever receptacle one has in mind. So, the canon is not really the list of included books; it is the principles (or, we might say, aesthetics) which allow for inclusion.

We seem somehow to have lost view of this etymology. The canon now is treated as if it were territory to be sacrificed for war reparations. "Okay, we the defeated forces of tradition agree to toss out old George Meredith (although we really sorta liked *The Ordeal of Richard Feveral*), and you can occupy his spot with Edith Wharton or Peewee Herman or whoever. Screw it. We give up." But nary a word is said by either side about why it was appropriate in the first place for George Meredith to be in every Victorian anthology or why it is good and proper for Edith Wharton to take his place. (Henry James would have kicked them both out, and for very particular reasons.)

Mere "inclusion" in a canon in which there is no *kanon*, or measuring stick, is a victory about as interesting as inclusion in a "prime-time fall lineup" of network television shows. It is a political victory, perhaps, but it allows in principle many kinds of stupidity. (Consider Amy Tan. Oh hell, consider *The Simpsons*. That's greatness, right? But compared to what?!) It would be far better to do away with the notion of a canon and insist instead on a shared understanding of the qualities of what we have called beauty, ethics, and meaning—that which we would choose to be the most advanced edge of our human project (which is a long way from being done if it is ever to be done "well"; everything hangs on that "well").

Now, none of this need imply that the social grievances of the canon-busters are not real. Sexism, racism, and homophobia are bloody real. The problem is that the very nature of the contest—competition for limited space within a "canon"—concedes an important victory to the opposition. The very idea that art is appropriately kept within a canon, what Adorno called a "cultural museum," is a tremendous victory for those who do not want art to be a destabilizing force. Canons stabilize. That's about the only thing they do well. Like the Middle Mind, the canon is a strategy for managing potentially radical energy. Insofar as academic feminists have placed the force of their work on the "politics of representation" in a heretofore male-dominated cultural canon, they have betrayed the original radical energy and promise of feminism. Fortunately, this energy lives on in artworks that are mostly outside the university. Putting the four astonishingly transgressive novels of British writer Ann Quin[3] in a "canon" does them no service at all. Her novels or Gabrielle Burton's *Heartbreak Hotel* or Pamela Zoline's *The Heat Death of the Universe* are still alive as fictions if they can continue to speak "autonomously," as Adorno put it, to readers. On the other hand, as correct as the politics of an Arundhati Roy may be (and I'm ready to say her politics are much more

---

[3] *Berg, Three, Tripticks,* and *Passages*, all published between 1964 and 1972. Quin died in 1973 at the age of thirty-seven.

right than wrong), as an *artist* her work begs for the canon. Her work frees no one from artistic convention, and it offers conservative forces considerable consolation because it maintains meaning as a function of "content" rather than form. As a consequence, winning the Great Canon Debate with writers like Roy is to lose a much larger battle.

In my judgment, John Guillory's *Cultural Capital* has said much of what I think needs to be said about the Great Canon Debate. His principal points seem to be that a) neither the side advocating the traditional canon nor the side representing the noncanonical understands the degree to which they participate in the construction of a "social imaginary" (in their depictions of, respectively, the traditional or the "repressed"); b) neither side quite recognizes how much they have in common (i.e., the assumption that canons are about social "values"); c) neither side understands the degree to which their debate takes place in "an ever shrinking island within the university itself"; and d) neither side understands that other, larger social forces—the culture of Jean-François Lyotard's postmodern "performativity," the technical literacy of the managerial class—have no stake and no interest in the debate. The professional managerial class has effectively devalued cultural literacy as a form of cultural capital and has replaced it with the needs of its own class: computer geeks to fix Y2K problems, for instance.[4]

Again, my interest in the canon debate has more to do with how it looks from the point of view of the one group involved in the production of the matter at hand but excluded from the debate: the artist, a practitioner involved in specific lineages of making certain kinds of things. The role of artists in this debate has been pretty much what the role of artists is in departments of English generally: idiot savant. So let

---

[4] This last point is elaborated with great acuity by Bill Readings in *The University in Ruins* under the concept of the "university of excellence." For Readings, the university is no longer the guarantor of a shared cultural tradition; it is, rather, the creator of manifold "excellences," most of which are quite marketable, thank you.

me pose the question in the name of artists. What should an artist's interest in the canon debate be?

To begin with, I think that the artist (you will excuse me for indulging in the construction of my own "social imaginary" here, as if there were only one perspective that could be said to be the artist's and that I for unspecified reasons know) is very dubious about the function of a canon. The artist has no interest in the traditionalist's "transmission of a legacy," in part because anyone can see what a self-serving line of baloney *that* one is, especially when delivered by ideological hacks such as William Bennett. On the other hand, the artist has little sympathy for the "minority" position that counter-canons should displace the dominant canon in this absurd zero-sum game that we seem determined to play. This is so because the artist has little sympathy for arguments about art that don't concern what is good, what is well done. The artist knows all too clearly what dull embarrassments can be made of mere political conviction or displays of virtue. For the artist, the "beautiful" is no mere idealist, essentialist premise; it is the necessity of every day's work. Without it there is no work and there certainly is no art. What troubles literary artists in particular is the idea that the most attentive segment of their audience, the professional literary critic, is unconcerned with what it means to make something well.

And so, as I was thinking about this question, it occurred to me that Guillory's book itself could provide insight into the problem, and could even reveal, perhaps, that the actions of scholars of both the left and the right speak louder than their positions. Because Guillory too is a maker of a particular sort of thing with its own lineage. So why would we say—as the panelists of the René Wellek Prize of the American Comparative Literature Association have concluded—that John Guillory's *Cultural Capital* is a good book, a book to be distinguished from the lot of unpublishable dissertations (of which there are many) and even distinguished from the lot of publishable manuscripts that are in spite of that fact not particularly good books (there are a lot of these too)? Why is his work of a quality that he deserves a seat on the faculty of the Johns Hopkins University and his book deserves to be published by the University of Chicago Press? Well, I read the book and I know why it's a good book, and I'm not a scholar in comparative literature. It's a good book because it's penetrating. It quickly goes beyond the cant that you might not ever have known you knew was cant until you read his book, and his arguments are sustained by a steady flow of original ideas. In fact, this book is loaded with ideas, if you know what those are. "Intelligence," like "beauty," is a theoretically discredited "essence" which we nonetheless live by, and I mean live by in absolutely the most serious and consequential sense. To live by something is to stake your life on it.

Guillory's book is an example of the qualities that ought to make something deserving of admission to a canon, if we must talk about canons, but which the *debate* over the canon doesn't know how to talk about. Guillory's work is in a tradition of literary, philosophical, and political analysis and argumentation that should be obscure to no one to whom that tradition is important. (How's that for a tautology?) It is as a tradition so important, in fact, that I would call it not merely an intellectual tradition but an ongoing and repeatedly emphasized proposition for what it should mean to be a human being. It is itself the proposition that intellectual penetration, an ability to express complex thoughts, to perform marvelous cognitive feats, and to break open experience in new and powerful ways, are fundamental human values. It is through these qualities that we will recognize what we call "intelligence."

For many centuries, frighteningly small, often embattled communities of human beings have been advancing this "imaginary" as that which the general culture *ought* to embrace because the culture *ought* to see that this sort of ability, this sort of performance is *deserving* of the notion of human capacity—that beleaguered capacity that the young Marx used to fret about, and upon which the rest of his powerful intellectual edifice is ethically balanced. But this doesn't seem to me to be how, in the present moment, we engage a book like Guillory's. We might agree with him, we might argue with his position, but we wouldn't think to say that what Guillory has performed is in itself a part of the debate. I'm not even sure that the René Wellek Award committee would see this.

And so, in spite of the fact that the canon has been reduced to arguments about the fairness of who is represented and who is not, academics continue to make judgments about the "good," whether that means grading student papers, writing book reviews, directing dissertations, making evaluations for publication, or selecting a book to be given an award. And one would like to hope that architects, builders of furniture, chefs, master gardeners, and other artists share the same regard for the "good" understood as the mastering and the moving forward of a specific tradition of human making. Only in this way is a world worthy of humans ultimately possible. This is something achieved only by individuals living in a world in which the imagination has real force.

Guillory quite comfortably accepts the assumptions of a particular kind of intellectual making as the premises by which he is willing to be judged. There is nothing unwise in this, either from my point of view or Guillory's. What his book acknowledges, in a way that is so familiar to intellectuals that it is nearly invisible, is that it has as a perhaps occluded value (but a value which it invests with the whole force of its performance) a set of assumptions about what it means to do something well. This is a stance that artists understand thoroughly and critics seem to have forgotten in principle if not in act.

We come here to the reality that the artist has most at heart. Artists understand what Jacques Derrida calls their "closure" intimately. The artist's closure is the accretion of individual artworks, of techniques and of traditions that allow artists to work and create in their own turn. This is what allows them to know in their bones that there is a difference between doing-what-artists-do well and doing-what-artists-do poorly. It is this historical certainty in the bone that prompted Henry James to wish for the death of the dilettante. The trick, of course, is to know what sort of claim to make for this closure, whether it be the closure of the artist (beauty) or that of the intellectual (intelligence). What we must not say is that "making well" is related to timeless, transcendental qualities. It is not about the conservative principle of the enduring and unchanging characteristics of a "common culture" of the best that has been thought and said. Making well is really a commitment to the absurd, because of the thoroughly contingent and historical genealogy (as Nietzsche would put it) of artistic making. And what we are really saying because we continue to *inhabit* those traditions through our productive practices is that *this* is our social imaginary. *This* is where we make our wager. *This*—to borrow art critic Dave Hickey's language—is where we should be trying to "win." Wanting to win goes beyond "making." Wanting to win reveals that the ultimate destination for artistic and intellectual making (in short, for the work of the imagination) is the proposing of an idea for what the human world should be.

For example, Mozart's and Beethoven's music argued against the tradition of classical formalism in the name of a new understanding of personal suffering, of indignation at that suffering, and generally of the importance of the subjective. Their music argued that the individual should stand for something both as a matter of social justice and as the beginning of a modern spirituality that culminated in Sören Kierkegaard's philosophy of religion and the individual. I hope that none of us, even after the end of the metaphysics of the subject, would want to entirely unsay that old Mozartian thought, or fail to appreciate the world that made it possible. Mozart lived in an authoritarian and repressive world, and yet the work of the imagination moved his world forward in profound ways. Is our own world so much more repressive than the Austro-Hungarian Empire, or so much better at controlling the work of the imagination that we cannot do something similar? Are we even capable of maintaining Mozart's imaginative revolution in the face of the ever-advancing National Security State?

3.

Let us see how the cultural right argues its position on the Great Canon Debate, now that I've used Professor Guillory to critique the academic left.

The lowest-common-denominator question in relation to the debate, asked with a whining impatience by a mostly nonexistent public (which is to say the terminally "not interested" public, the severe and profoundly distracted public), is, "Are the great books great or not?" But this is of course a television question. This is what Oprah asks her adoring audience, doe-eyed with sincerity. This is, in short, the sort of thing that inquiring minds want to know. Nonetheless, I for one am happy to answer that, yes, the great works were and are great, whatever that means (and it means very little; a good old-fashioned tautology is what it is, just the sort of tautology that made this country great).

But, as we should know, there is another question that needs to be asked, a question that takes us beyond tautology. The question is, "Of what does the greatness of the great works consist?" Hearing this question, you can feel North America's inquiring minds go, "Uh-oh," in anticipation that this is the sort of question that opens the door to just the people they don't want to hear from, who also happen to be just the people whose professional responsibility it is to answer the question: professors. For this is not only an aesthetic question, it is an epistemological question. How do we know what we think we know about the beautiful and the great? Uh-oh, indeed.

And yet the question "Of what does the greatness of the great works consist?" is exactly the *right* question, and if the deconstructive critical lineage has had no other positive contributions to make to contemporary thought, it has posed this fundamental aesthetic/epistemological question and then fairly warned, "Do not answer with a tautology, or through vaporous metaphysics, or the wish-fulfillment of ideology." Frankly, there have not been many responses worthy of the deconstructive challenge, although there are responses that should be available to us (as I've mentioned already in connection with Adorno). It is in part because of the vacuum created by the thoroughness of deconstruction's critique of aesthetic metaphysics, that those of what Harold Bloom calls the School of Resentment have had the opportunity to de-aestheticize literary criticism and, worse yet, de-aestheticize our expectations of literary texts. It's as if we're being told, "If you can't tell me why the aesthetic should matter without revealing yourself for hopelessly metaphysical or hopelessly Republican, I sure as hell can tell you why sexism, racism, homophobia, and imperialism matter." The unhappy consequence of this argument, for those of us who think that art should matter, is the conclusion that the least important aspect of a work of art is precisely its artfulness.

So, I would propose to try, as we all should try, to understand what it is that makes for the greatness of the great, but before I do so I need to say a brief something about what the greatness of the great does *not* rest on. It does not rest on William Bennett's assertion that the great is great because "it is the best that has been thought and said." The greatness of the great does not and cannot rest on a question-begging platitude.

Certainly the most notable attempt to save an essentially conservative position from a dependency on platitude has been the recent work of Harold Bloom, *The Western Canon* in particular. Unfortunately, in this work Bloom has taken far less care than he should have to make important discriminations about the thought of deconstruction or of feminism or of postmodernism. Rather, he lumps them into one monstrous and threatening whole, just like any Reagan-Bush hack, called variously the School of Resentment or simply (when he's feeling very mean-spirited, the well-paid champion of rightwing pundits everywhere) "cheerleaders." He also strongly implies, just as Bennett, Dinesh D'Souza, Roger Kimball, George Will, Lynne Cheney, and others have done, that we are in a moment of crisis and that theorists, postmodernists, feminists, and multiculturalists are to blame for it. He also simplifies and misrepresents crucial ideas, like the Death of the Author, to suit his own polemical purpose. The point of the critique of the idea of Author was never to claim that someone named William Shakespeare didn't exist (heaven forfend!) or didn't write his plays or doesn't deserve "credit" for them (may it serve him well). Rather, the concept of the Death of the Author was a way of showing something any artist knows: that the sublimely unified self of Romantic genius was always already contaminated by that which was not-self. In short, artists are dependent upon the artists who preceded them.

Here Bloom joins the hysterical right wing and does a profound disservice to what is in its own terms legitimately "great" about the thought of Michel Foucault and Jacques Derrida in particular. The most disturbing aspect of this is that, unlike with D'Souza, you suspect that Bloom *knows* he is misrepresenting, that he understands more than he allows, as the colleague and friend of Paul de Man should. (Or are we obliged to imagine long, painful evenings *chez* de Man, New Haven, circa 1975, in which de Man thinks to himself, "This poor son of a bitch really doesn't get it!")

In Bloom's less frenzied moments, he does make a good-faith effort to account for the greatness of the great, inadequate though that argument is from my perspective. I would like to follow his logic on two principal concepts that form the bedrock of his defense of the canon: the "anxiety of influence" and the "uncanny."

Bloom writes, in *The Western Canon*, "Poems, stories, novels, plays come into being as a response to prior poems, stories, novels and plays, and that response depends upon acts of reading and interpretation by the later writers, acts that are identical with the new works." (9)

Fair enough, but there's more. This influence of the work of the past becomes an "agon," a competition, for the writers of the present. For the would-be canonical writers experience anxiety not only about their relationship to the talents and the works of the past but also about their own mortality. Thus, to join the canon means to compete not only with the past but also with the present in a drive for the qualified immortality of joining the canon and thereby joining what Bloom calls "communal memory."

The principal means through which writers win their agonistic struggle with the past and win out over the fear of their own mortality is through "originality," what the reader experiences as the "uncanny." The uncanny is not a quantifiable quality. As Bloom says, "Aesthetic value can be recognized or experienced, but it cannot be conveyed to those who are incapable of grasping its sensations and perceptions." (17) (Isn't this a gussied-up version of the Lovin' Spoonful's claim that, "I'd like to tell you 'bout the magic that can free your soul, but it's like trying to tell a stranger 'bout rock 'n' roll"? Isn't it, in short, a mystification?)

On the other side, the reader's side, reading, for Bloom, is the "proper use of one's solitude," a "solitude whose final form is one's confrontation with one's mortality." (19) In *How to Read and Why,* Bloom writes, "Imaginative literature is otherness, and as such alleviates loneliness. We read not only because we cannot know enough people, but because friendship is so vulnerable, so likely to diminish or disappear, overcome by space, time, imperfect sympathies, and all the sorrows of familial and passional life." (19)

Passional?

I find it difficult to see how such a formulation is much of an improvement over William Bennett's platitudes. In this form, literature ought also to appeal to people who like snuggly kittens. Is Bloom simply saying what he appears to be saying, that books are our friends and our good friends the books (not just any old book, of course, but our *best* friends the masterpieces, whatever they are; they're what Professor Bloom says they are, apparently) stand by our side till the very end so that we're not afraid to die? Is that it?

Over the last thirty-five years there has never been a moment when I, for one, was not reading one to five books at a time, and yet it has never seemed to me that I read primarily because I was lonely. I read for the same reason that I listened to music, because it was interesting, pleasurable, and I always felt I was becoming "larger," or more fully human, because of it. Reading is an expression not of "loneliness" but of a very different human emotion (if we must deal in primary human emotions): curiosity. Reading is a part of our desire for experience, a desire to know the world, to internalize the world, to prepare to judge the world, and even to be able to participate in the future construction of that world. With respect to art and intellect, it's not so much that one is afraid of dying but that one is afraid of dying *empty.*

There is also a curious logic afoot in Bloom's rendering of the interests of writers in relation to the interests of readers. Writers use their "originality" to achieve immortality. Does this say something very pleasant about writers? The fundamental incentive behind their efforts is the dubious perpetuation of their egos ensconced in the canon? Is this something we should admire them for? Is it a healthy thing or a symptom of a cultural pathology (fame)? As the veteran of many a writing seminar, I've seen plenty of writerly egos in my time, but it has never occurred to me that our vainglorious lust for never-vast-enough recognition was the basis for something we should be admired for, let alone the basis for the greatness of the authentically literary. Rather, it uniformly struck me as an ego delusion, a delusion that, moreover, helps us very little in understanding the greatness of the greatest works of art.

And on the reader's side, why is the reader interested in the uncanny (a.k.a. "originality")? Why is the uncanny interesting? Okay, writers achieve immortality through originality—I can follow that (simplistic though it may be)—but what exactly does the uncanny offer readers? A *frisson*? And how does the leading aesthetic effect of uncanniness lead the reader, as Bloom claims, to a confrontation with mortality? Does the uncanny somehow make the reader less lonely?

Harold Bloom is quite right to be disturbed by the de-aestheticizing of literature produced by the sociologizing of literary criticism on the race-class-gender axis. And he is quite right to claim that art's purpose is not the display of social virtues. But his own proposals for why the aesthetic *should* count, and especially count for those works in the Western canon, are self-congratulatory, platitudinous, and . . . fusty.

It is striking that Harold Bloom's notion of the uncanny is not uncanny itself. In fact, it should seem quite familiar to us. The conceptual basis of his defense of the canon is an account of the relationship between tradition and innovation. What is startling is the fact that Bloom makes so little use of the theoretical work that has been done on the role of innovation in the arts. What I would propose to do is revisit the thinking of Viktor Shklovsky, Russian formalist of the 1930s, in order to construct an approach to aesthetics that responds to what Bloom and many others, myself included, see as an impoverished moment in the history of literary criticism.

One of the most conspicuous places in which we can see the work of something like Bloom's notion of the uncanny is in Shklovsky's concept of "enstrangement" (in Benjamin Sher's translation). But with what a difference. Shklovsky shared with Martin Heidegger a concern about human perception and its relationship to what it means to be a full human being. For both, language as the prose-of-life or as referential instrument is insufficient to perception's human need. Shklovsky wrote, "If we examine the general laws of perception, we see that as it becomes habitual, it also becomes automatic. . . . Automization eats away at things, at clothes, at furniture, at our wives, and at our fear of war." (5) Both Shklovsky and Heidegger sought to oppose poetry to prose for the purpose of the return of perception, for the refreshing of the language that captures perception, and ultimately for the clarifying of our very humanity.

Shklovsky wrote, "And so, in order to return sensation to our limbs, in order to make us feel objects, to make a stone feel stony, man has been given the tool of art." (6)

The restoration of those capacities that are most innately human is accomplished through "enstrangement." Enstrangement seeks to emancipate the work from the leaden forms of the past by describing things as if seen for the first time, by telling stories from unusual points of view, or by placing things out of context. Most broadly, enstrangement is at work whenever an image leads us "to a 'vision' of this object rather than a mere 'recognition.'" (10)

What should be clear from this brief description is that, contrary to Harold Bloom's account, the artistic, social, and human motivation for artist and audience is shared and consequential. We are not talking about an agon whose triumph over tradition is its own hollow thrill of victory, but a triumph whose purpose is the generalization for both reader and writer of the aesthetic experience understood as the quintessence of human experience. And we are certainly not talking in some vague way about a therapeutic consolation for the vagaries of the "passional" life. As for the proponents of a criticism on the race-class-gender axis, Shklovsky's lesson is simple: the art of enstrangement itself is the most consequential social act. It is what art has to give, without apology, to the social.

Shklovsky also calls forcefully to our attention the importance of "complexity" and "difficulty." Why, one might ask, is the greatness of a work often tied to its complexity? Is it because complexity makes one feel less lonely? Or less mortal? The difference between a simple folk melody or a hymn and the work of art that a Bach or Beethoven will then make of this tune is simply that the artwork is vastly more complex. Both the folk tune and the Beethoven sonata ultimately confirm the same laws of tonality and harmonics of the diatonic. The difference is that Beethoven will test the limits of the diatonic, or work against the expectations of the diatonic for dramatic effect, or even leave that confine for brief and startling moments. We admire Beethoven and his fellow adventurers for this, and hold them to be "great," in part because our culture admires the performance of difficult feats. But we also admire such complexity because it seems to be telling us something both truer and more complete about the world in which we live. The Beethoven sonata is more adequate to our sense of the real than the simple folk tune. As Frank Kermode argued in his book *The Sense of an Ending*, artistic innovation tends to abandon, complexify, or subvert conventional formal expectations. When encountering innovative fiction, we "feel that the fiction under consideration is one of those which, by upsetting the ordinary balance of our naive expectations, is finding something out for us, something *real.*" (18) This is not to say that there is anything wrong with or lacking in the folk tune, but it is to say that Beethoven's rendering and extending of its premises is much more emotionally and intellectually rich. Beethoven's version seeks to be larger and more encompassing. It is more ambitious.[5]

---

[5] It's worth acknowledging here that we are indeed close to the New Critical aestheticism of Monroe Beardsley. Beardsley argued that an aesthetic object has complexity, intensity, and unity. Unlike Shklovsky, Beardsley detached these artistic qualities from ordinary life. Although it is true that Beardsley's "detachment" is now substantially and correctly discredited, it is remarkable that as a practical matter we continue to judge the success and worth of literature by his criteria. As I said in relation to Guillory's work, these *de facto* habits of judgment speak louder than our formal rejection of the systems from which the judgments first emerged. Complexity, intensity, and unity are theoretically discredited qualities that we nonetheless continue to live by.

Shklovsky pushes this understanding of complexity by introducing the aesthetic force of "difficulty." We could say simply that difficulty comes with complexity, but Shklovsky would remind us that difficulty is also about the risk of moving outside of the familiar, outside of the diatonic, outside of what Derrida likes to call our "closure." The virtue of the difficult, or what we often call the "experimental," is that it keeps the necessary stability of our "closure" (which we surely need in order to share a common culture and live together in it), but it keeps that closure from becoming something deadening. *The problem that art helps us face, and great art helps us face best, is the problem of creating social stability without creating a state of administered conformity.* In other words, art helps us to think what it would mean to live together as a whole and yet be fully human as individuals.

My point in this partial reprisal of Shklovsky's thought is to reveal how close Bloom comes, in his notion of the uncanny, to saying something very central to aesthetic experience while managing at the same time to utterly miss the mark. Bloom's concept is merely mystifying, but Shklovsky helps us to see that it is possible to imagine a more powerful human and, yes, social function for the uncanny understood as the enstranging force of innovation. But this has nothing to do with competition for inclusion in a canon. In Shklovsky's vision, the imagination works through art to exploit the opportunity that enstrangement has provided. The imagination makes the world bloom through the moment of enstrangement. Shklovsky's own stunning and mostly unread novel *Zoo: Or Letters Not About Love* is testimony to this possibility.

It may be a clarifying (if scandalous) example of the artistic and social force of enstrangement to recall that many of the musical and visual artists of the 1960s, especially the graphic poster artists around the Fillmore and Avalon Ballrooms in San Francisco, understood the chemical "enstrangement" of LSD as the opportunity for a kind of art that had simply never existed before, uniting high art with mass culture. As graphic artist Bob Schnepf tells it in a 2002 interview by Dan Craft in the December 26, 2002, *Bloomington-Normal Pantagraph*, "I was taking visions I had perceived through the use of mind-altering substances. For me, personally, it was what opened the door of perception and it started me seeing things in a different way. I could have stopped after the first couple experiences and still arrived at my vision, because once the door was opened, I could find my way from that point on." Like Shklovsky's purely aesthetic enstrangement (although this too depends on just how much absinthe he was drinking in Paris during his years in exile from the Soviet Union), Schnepf's account of his development is about perception and about breaking with the dead forms of the past in order to see as if for the first time.

For these artists, acid broke through the crust of the quotidian that Wallace Stevens labored against (without chemical assistance) and opened up the opportunity for the imagination to create audacious claims on its world. To live in the San Francisco Bay Area at that time, as I did, and to see those colorful posters with their bizarre appeal stuck up on street corners and handed out at concerts was to experience an utterly rare thing: the imagination driving art to the creation of a new human world, a world whose defining principle was open possibility. Needless to say, getting "experienced," as Jimi Hendrix put it, in order to open these doors of perception and possibility is better and more safely done through art and thought than through drugs. But in a culture as homogenized and repressive as ours was in the early 1960s, it's not a wonder that the arrival of LSD suddenly and radically exploded that lusterless world and stimulated so much deviation not only in the acidified art world but in its huge young audience.

Let me put the question in this way: Do you get "Purple Haze" and the work of the Jimi Hendrix Experience without drugs? No, without drugs you get the Isley Brothers, which is not bad but it isn't something that sends a jolt through youth consciousness for the next quarter-century. The "experience" was not simply the crude sensation of taking drugs; it was the experience of seeing things "enstranged" or, as Walter Benjamin put it, with an "aura." The "experience" was, in a no doubt hyperbolic mode, the amber light or jar on a hill in

Tennessee with which I began this book. It cut through the crust of the ordinary, dissolved the normal, and altered our sense of what ought to happen. Of course, many artists, Hendrix included, failed to see that the drug itself was not the point. Many would-be artists quickly fell victim to the "Drunkspeare" syndrome, in which chemical intoxication becomes the point of being an artist. But after Hendrix, people could, and people still do, find in his art the enstrangement that allows them to wonder about the possibilities not only for music per se but for what Hendrix's music implies about the kind of world we should live in. It continues to suggest something very different from what BMG and Sony have in mind for our global life together—and this in spite of the conspicuous efforts to create halls of fame and museums to domesticate and sanitize his disruptive vision. Thirty years later, there is still something radically suggestive about the work of a Schnepf or a Hendrix, just as there is still something, as Adorno points out, radical and disruptive about Beethoven if you can find it beneath the varnish of civic virtue with which his work has been layered for the last two centuries. What remains for me disconcerting and disappointing is the lack of sensitivity to these powers in art among both radical and conservative academics. They have controlled the discourse about art and literature for the last thirty years, but they understand little about art's fundamental force and promise. As Wallace Stevens wrote in the poem "Poetry Is a Destructive Force,"

> *The lion sleeps in the sun.*
> *Its nose is on its paws.*
> *It can kill a man.*

I think we've lost any sense of this raw power of the imagination. Certainly, the institutions we've charged with its maintenance and care have no clue at all about this power. They've given themselves over to an understanding of the imagination appropriate either for sociologists or for lugubrious fetishists of dead "legacies." In the absence of the imaginative ferment of what Schnepf describes as three brief years in one small place during which creative energy was supreme, drug-driven or not, our world has only been all the more at the mercy of the all-too-predictable purposes of politicians and their corporate sponsors in pursuit of their ideal: a world closed and defined by technological rationality. It is to this world and its most recent manifestations that I turn next.

Chapter 3

THE GREAT AMERICAN
DISASTER MACHINE

> Boy, we're sure going to have some wrecks now!
> Walt Disney, upon setting up the
> model train set that circled his house

1.

We have to this point discovered the poverty of the American imagination where one might expect it, in the world of the Middle Mind, and we have discovered it in the perhaps less likely world of academia, especially in the social criticism of Cultural Studies and Harold Bloom's rightwing ideology. It is time now to look at the poverty of the imagination in its broadest venue: the political narratives of the United States as created by our political leaders and their comrades in the media, in technology, and in business.[1] Here the implications of the poverty of the imagination are starkest and most deadly. This particular poverty, because of its context, is only just short of apocalyptic, and in the long run we may find that it is simply apocalyptic *tout court*. Perhaps we will find that our failure in the world of politics is our ultimate failure. Our last and most fateful failure.

---

[1] I would add to this list of comrades the military, but the truth is that we don't really hear much from them, unless a military unit is unfortunate enough to take out a boat full of Japanese students, or a ski lift, briefly scandalizing the world. Politicians do the work of justifying the military's existence and justifying the 50 percent of the discretionary federal budget that the military gobbles up, leaving all of 8 percent to education. So the military can afford to be strong and silent. They're professional killers, you see. They don't do talk.

We will also find in looking at the American political imagination that it is only a sort of puppet show for the real work of another kind of imagination. When we think about the appalling transparency of the narratives created by Ronald Reagan and Presidents Bush the First and Second, or when we consider these leaders' preposterous melodramas about the Nicaraguan contras, Noriega as Hitler, Saddam Hussein as Satan, or Iran, Iraq, and North Korea as an Axis of Evil, it's hard to take them seriously as fictions, let alone as objective propositions about the world. And in fact it may well be that these narratives, farcical as they are, function merely as a sort of sleight of hand, obscuring the more consequential work of the imagination which goes on in a different but closely related area of national discourse.

The work of Paul Virilio, to which I will turn first, reveals that what we have taken for the work of politics is at its foundation the work of the technological imagination, beginning in the military (as the World Wide Web did) and ending as the motor of profit in the new global economy. If we want to understand our political future, we need to understand where technology in its relationship with capitalism and the military is taking us. Rather than reading the *Washington Post* and wondering, the day after the 2002 State of the Union Address, whether Bush really meant that crapola about the Axis of Evil, we need to be reading *Wired*, where all of the narratives and all of the intoxicated speculation is quite earnest, quite smart, and deadly real. As imagination, it is all too convincing.

The most familiar and recent creations of our political imagination are the characterizations of the crisis of "September 11" and the "War Against Terror." These narratives suffer from an inability to think beyond a truth that is persuasive because it is also trite. I hope I need say very little, in this regard, about the script that 90 percent of the nation has been following (if our friends the pollsters at CNN, Gallup, and elsewhere are to be believed). America has been attacked; we're "at war with terrorism"; but "America will strike back," because we're a "beacon of freedom to the rest of the world," because "innocent people lost their lives," because "America has lost its innocence," because there are "evildoers" afoot. We'll "smoke them out of their holes," because our cause is just and we are united. After two years, there is still substantial credence given to these proposi- tions, and there is little sign of a "credibility gap" of the type we ex- perienced during the war in Vietnam, with its "domino theory" of Communist aggression.

The idea that CNN is right and 90 percent of the populace con- tinues to believe this palaver is perhaps more frightening than the threat of receiving a suspicious piece of mail postmarked New Jersey. The odds of receiving anthrax in the mail (or a pipe bomb from an un- dergraduate art major from Wisconsin, one of America's own pure products gone crazy) are statistically minute, but the yahoos with Old Glory rippling from the roofs of their suburban assault vehicles are ev- erywhere, bearing who knows what malice for those lacking proper pa- triotic fervor. Much worse and more dangerous than this, of course, are organizations like the American Council of Trustees and Alumni, formed in 2001 by Lynne Cheney and Joseph Lieberman. For this group, any movement away from the grossly patriotic is a "failing." They would save American culture by removing from it any thought that isn't utterly conformist with the opinion of "the public at large." (Doesn't the fact that Cheney and Lieberman are in sync on this issue say something depressing about our democratic choices in the last election?) With attorneys general like John Ashcroft, the possibility that such a desire could acquire legal teeth through "anti-terrorism" legislation is frighteningly real. Like a persecutor, some McCarthyist nightmare of the 1950s, Ashcroft has made it his business to know what books we check out of the library[2] and what sites we visit on the

---

[2] The USA Patriot Act, overwhelmingly approved by our Congress (a body for which discretion is always the better part of valor), obliges your librarians to inform on you if the FBI or Homeland Security asks what you've been reading lately. Just hope that *Jane's Encyclopedia of Military Aircraft* wasn't on your reading list this summer. Oh, I know I've made you curious and now you want to read *Jane's*, but, please, exer- cise some forbearance. It's for your own sake and your country's that I ask this.

Internet—all in the name of national security. As William Safire described it in the *New York Times* (November 14, 2002),

> Every purchase you make with a credit card, every magazine subscription you buy and medical prescription you fill, every Web site you visit and e-mail you send or receive, every academic grade you receive, every bank deposit you make, every trip you book and every event you attend, all these transactions and communications will go into what the Defense Department describes as "a virtual, centralized grand database."

We are now, in alternation, either the United Crisis States of America or the United Security States of America. Crisis and Security call to each other, one upping the other's ante, spiraling, the crises growing graver, the security more extreme.

But there is also poverty in the leftwing critique of the events related to 9-11 and the war in Iraq. The leftwing critique seeks to create a historical and geopolitical context for understanding the "tensions in the region." Thus, the roots of al-Qaeda are in nineteenth-century colonialism and Cold War meddling in Islamic countries (read: oil-producing countries) by a U.S. foreign policy premised on the idea that we have "national interests" in the region upon which depends what President Bush has called our "sacred lifestyle." Hence, it is a "foreign policy priority" to "stabilize" certain Middle Eastern client states, whether putatively democratic or plainly autocratic. Our real antagonist here, as Noam Chomsky argues in his little book *9-11* (2001), is the reservoir of bitterness and anger over U.S. policies in the region.

Needless to say, there is a lot more credibility in this latter vision of the world. It's the "America as imperial power" point of view developed over many decades of analysis by Noam Chomsky, *The Nation*, and the South End Press. But more accurate though this version of things may be, its truth-power is also dependent on its familiarity. It's not as if the left has ever been immune to what Stuart Hall called the need for the "narrative construction of reality." It's just that the left construction is not a naked expression of economic self-interest. But in the final analysis, to say that the United States is an imperialist country and leave it at that denies our present reality much-needed gradations of hue. Our situation may be dark, but it isn't simply the familiar black of a nineteenth-century empire-builder.

A digression here: Chalmers Johnson's book *Blowback* (2000) offers a provocative third option (situated between the Bush administration party line and the left's critique of that line) and qualified hope for a broad alternative to current political assumptions. Johnson's book is a detailed account of what he calls, bluntly, American imperialism. His descriptions of how our actions have created global resentment, and "blowback" consequences for ourselves because of that resentment, rival Chomsky's most detailed accounts of our foreign military and economic interventions. But Johnson is also a mainstream intellectual, and he is always careful to confine his analyses within the context of the assumption that the United States is a "peace-loving" country and a true democracy that has been betrayed by its own leaders, by its economic elite, and by a military apparatus gone rogue.

Apparently, according to Johnson, the American public has "plausible deniability." We didn't know. We were out of the loop. The question, of course, as the popular press likes to put it, is "What did we know, and when?"

The idea that there is any sense in which the American public could be said not to know what we do is finally not credible. Are we dupes of propaganda? Is the truth censored? To a degree the answer to both of those questions is yes. It's not as if the network news folks are eager to help us put together a diagnosis of our imperial objectives and methods. But the weightier answer is that we operate under a New Censorship which functions by making everything known and naked to a paralyzing degree. Is there anyone who doesn't understand that the Sudanese pharmaceutical lab that Clinton blew up with eighty cruise missiles was producing . . . pharmaceuticals? Is there anyone who doesn't understand that this was an act of state terrorism and a violation of every principle of international law? We will pillory and impeach a president for getting a blow job literally "in office" (a scenario most honest fifty-something males will envy wistfully), but an utterly irresponsible act of militarism with who knows what consequences for the patients who will now not be able to receive the drugs the factory produced—well, this is something that needs to be pondered. Clinton was, after all, looking after national interests, was he not? Should Clinton have been impeached? Bet your ass. But not for anything having to do with a certain cherubic brunette, a vision out of the paintings of Peter Paul Rubens. Clinton emerged unscathed from this crime against the people of the Sudan because of a) racism (the unspoken assumption being that it's okay to bomb little brown people—it happens so often, they ought to be used to it by now; it's rather like the weather for them), b) the unacknowledged understanding that American military activities really do support our privileges stateside, such as those privileges are, and c) the stupefying effects of the New Censorship.

The New Censorship does not work by keeping things secret. Are our leaders liars and criminals? Is the government run by wealthy corporations and political elites? Are we all being slowly poisoned? The answer is yes to all of the above, and there's hardly a soul on these shores who doesn't know it. The reign of George II practically revels in this perverse transparency. Oil policy created in backrooms with lobbyists from Enron and Exxon-Mobil. Naked pandering to the electricity industry in rolling back clean-air mandates. Accounting firms like Arthur Andersen buying even "watchdog" liberal senators such as Christopher Dodd. Elections rigged with brother Jeb's connivance in Florida. All of these details are utterly public, reported in newspapers, television newscasts, and books, yet it's perfectly safe for this stuff to be known. The genius of the New Censorship is that it works through the obscenity of absolute openness. Iraq-gate wasn't a secret. The real secret is that it wasn't a secret, and certainly wasn't a scandal. It was business as usual. The betrayal of public trust is a daily story manipulated by the media within the narrative confines of "scandal," when in fact it's all a part of the daily routine and everyone knows it. The media makes pornography of the collective guilt of our politicians and business leaders. They make a yummy fetish of betrayed trust. We then consume it, mostly passively, because it is indistinguishable from our "entertainment" and because we suspect in some dim way that, bad as it surely is, it is working in our interests in the long run. What genius to have a system that allows you to behave badly, be exposed for it, and then have the sin recouped by the system as a sellable commodity! I mean, you have to admire the sheer, recuperative balls of it!

All this being the case, what consequences can we expect from the work of Chalmers Johnson or Noam Chomsky? None. Their writings are taken up as part of the spectrum (a modestly disturbing part of that spectrum, to be sure) of info-pornographics. The truth-function of Chomsky's work is neutralized because there are people who will participate in actions leading to death and worse all over the world and then tell you about it. In detail. In great detail. The truth is that everything is known, the revelation grotesquely vivid. Turn Salvadoran death-squad commanders into millionaires for killing peasants? We do that. It's called the Fort Benning School of the Americas. There's a budget line for it every year. Every year you pay for it. It's a crime without consequences. By any traditional standard, the United States is a corrupt society because it refuses to be responsible before ethical facts that it knows perfectly well. This is corruption: after years of disgraceful shilly-shally, in the spring of 2002 the administration of George II acknowledged that there is a scientific basis to global warming but that there is nothing to be done about it (or nothing to be done that wouldn't piss off Detroit, Exxon-Mobil, and so-called "soccer moms," who are now, according to Republicans, the wild card in national energy politics). So, we'll just have to adapt. Truth without consequences is a good working definition of corruption. Only the bizarre "unconsciousness" provided by the New Censorship, where everything awful is pink and in your face, allows this corruption a shred of cover.

Let's return to the possibilities offered by the pronouncements of the Bush administration and the Chomskian left. In the shock of the days after the World Trade Center disaster, I felt at times that both the patriotic and the leftwing analyses were sufficient, and sometimes my alarm was such that both seemed persuasive at the same time. We were attacked, after all. Any state, even an imperialist state with no plausible claim to innocence (for when was there ever an innocent state?), has the right and the obligation to defend its citizens. That's why it's good to live in scary Leviathan, as Thomas Hobbes conceived it. Leviathan protects you from other Leviathans. It's a "necessary evil" argument.

So, as an exercise in imagination remediation, I decided to reread Paul Virilio's *Pure War* (1983), a book which combines social, political, and military analysis with a unique and encompassing vision of the real that qualifies, for me, as an act of the imagination. I then thought I could use Virilio's ideas for the purpose of reimagining the world implied in the "recent events."

Virilio argues that the history of Western societies is really the history of their militaries. The social hardly counts at all for him except as a consequence of the military. According to Virilio, we have moved on from a time in which we had simple War, which was limited and tactical. War was once something that happened outside of the moat or city wall or Maginot Line, on this side of which civilian life went its way with its own priorities. War gave way to Total War, which overwhelmed the entirety of the social system as well as the economic and industrial capacity of the state because of the need for ever-faster, ever-more-powerful war technology, and because of the need to supply the logistical demands of its dispersed military presence. Total War was about logistics, not battlefield tactics. The American Civil War inaugurated Total War, and the two world wars fulfilled it. It was industrial capacity and transportation, not brilliant military tactics, that allowed the North to win the Civil War.

Beyond Total War is Pure War. In Pure War the state is on an implicit war footing even in times of peace. (I suppose we know this condition best as the Cold War, but I suspect we will soon see an even purer example of it in President Bush's War Against Terror, the "task that never ends.") Technology, the media, industrial production, the economy, and certainly politics are first about a war so diffuse and ubiquitous that few people even recognize it for what it is. Hence, the *trompe l'oeil* in our current situation is the appearance that the hot war in Iraq is categorically different from the peace which preceded it. This, of course, means that we are asked to believe that we are still citizens of the nineteenth century and that our campaign against Saddam and al-Qaeda is purely tactical. This is a description of a poverty of imagination with the most dire consequences, because it commits us to continue on a course that all but ensures that there will be future terrorist tragedies on our own ground.

Perhaps the most frightening aspect of this situation is the near dead certainty that not only are our middle-class flag-wavers living in utter misrecognition, but it is likely that the leaders of our country (from George II to Teddy K) are every bit as deluded and, moreover, impotent. Randy Hayes of the Rainforest Action Network once told me of a talk he had with the über-CEO of the Mitsubishi Company. Hayes said he was able to convince this CEO that Mitsubishi's program of global devastation for short-term profit was not in the long-term interest of either the planet or the company. Hayes achieved this moment of clarity only to have it followed by a far larger and more monstrous clarity for both himself and the Mitsubishi head: Mr. Mitsubishi had no idea how to change the practices of the company, because the logic that drove the company was both systemic and autonomous. This system at which even CEOs must look with apocalyptic horror is part of the ecology of Pure War and is not available for political discussion, let alone democratic debate. In short, it is not responsive to the will or the interests of the human beings living within it. Virilio calls this situation the "State as Destiny."

Let's look at a few passages from *Pure War* to see what sort of light they might shed on our current situation. First, "In the end, unconsciousness is the aim of Pure War." (124) In the *Grundrisse* Karl Marx argued that one of the most conspicuous products of capitalism is stupidity. There is no shortage of stupidity around at present. Still,

Virilio's idea that we're "unconscious" (rather than stupid) has more explanatory power. Unconscious in what sense? North Americans are not speaking to their culture; they're being spoken by it. (As I've said, this is a curious sort of "unconsciousness" which functions in the context of a lurid revelation of all, the brutal exposure of everything. The better way of thinking of it might be the unconsciousness of the pure and passive "spectator," to borrow from the vocabulary of Guy Debord's *Society of the Spectacle.* The spectator sees all but takes responsibility for nothing.) The media is a function of the war effort, foreclosing on all deviant perspectives, constantly reaffirming the orthodox rubbish we think we already know.

And certainly we are "unconscious" in the sense that we are so blithely irresponsive to, if not unaware of, the fact that our "lifestyle" has for the last half-century been the equivalent of a state of war between ourselves and those folks who will provide us cheap, cheap natural resources and, more recently, cheap, cheap consumer goods or pay the price. This is emphatically true of people in the Middle East, who have been told, essentially, "You will suffer the injustice and indignity of a military-client-state-of-last-resort (Israel) established in your midst by Western fiat.[3] You will suffer and live in poverty in spite of the opulence of your rulers, who will rule at least in part because we guarantee them. And in return you will give us cheap oil so that General Motors and Big Oil can continue to profit, Americans can drive any sort of steel nightmare they like, and metropolitan areas can be organized around the great suburban principle 'Get in your car or stay home.'" (And while I'm on the subject of getting in the family sedan, what the

---

[3] Churchill on the rights of Palestinians: "I do not agree that the dog in a manger has the final right to the manger even though he may have lain there for a very long time. I do not admit that right. I do not admit, for instance, that a great wrong has been done to the Red Indians of America or the black people of Australia. I do not admit that a wrong has been done to these people by the fact that a stronger race, a higher grade race, a more worldly wise race to put it that way, has come in and taken their place." (quoted in Roy) So much for the great fighter against Nazi theories of race!

hell is the rest of the world supposed to make of the fact that we were instructed by our commander-in-chief to help in the "war effort" against terrorism by shopping? Afghanis are fleeing for the borders, dodging bombs, and we're doing our bit by heading out to the mall? Is this the postmodern version of WWII ration cards and neighborhood rubber and metal drives?)

More from Virilio:

> The military class is turning into an internal super-police. . . .
> In the strategy of deterrence, military institutions, no longer fighting among themselves, tend to fight only civilian societies—with, of course, a few skirmishes in the Third World. (94)

Another critical aspect of our perpetual war-readiness, about which Pure War's domestic accomplices are largely unconscious, is the idea that these patriotic citizens are themselves enduring victims of "endo-colonization." We have internalized the military and its imperatives. We police ourselves, as Michel Foucault famously argued. This is most distressingly the case in the sense that the vitality of the human world has been conquered by the internalization of technology as an extension of the military. Virilio writes:

> Movement is now only a handicap [;] . . . that we know only too well. A motor-handicap: a man in a car piloted by a driver (until such time as cars are completely automatic, which won't take long) is *motor*-handicapped. . . . The man sitting before his television watching the soccer championship live from Santiago in Chile is *seeing*-handicapped. . . . Now, the prostheses of automotive-audio-visual movement create a subliminal comfort. Subliminal, meaning beyond consciousness. They allow a kind of visual—thus physical—hallucination, which tends to strip us of our consciousness. Like the "I run for you" of automobile technology, an "I *see* for you" is created. (75)

These technological prostheses are, for Virilio, completely alienating. And yet they are at the heart of what our involvement in the Middle East is really about. One could put the perverse truth of the matter in these crude terms: *we must make war to ensure the continuance of a social and economic system that dehumanizes people by making them dependent upon machines.* The obvious instance here is the relationship of past, present, and future wars in the Middle East to the maintenance of what we quaintly call "car culture." But the car is only part of what our "sacred lifestyle" involves. I've been wondering lately what would happen if you could force these issues to consciousness and resolve them through a democratic and political process. I think that the key issue for this imaginary plebiscite would essentially be this:

Okay, in order to have a moral and peaceful relationship with the rest of the world, especially the Third World, we will need to radically reimagine urban and suburban space so that it is not all about accommodating the automobile; we will need to accept less prosperity in the form of discretionary income to purchase consumer items because we will need to let more of the wealth generated by the work of people in the Third World stay in Bangladesh and the *maquiladoras* of Mexico; we will need to radically reduce our dependence on our cars; and we will need to stop thinking of ourselves as the one great military (and nuclear) exception in world relations. We will also need to do the work to wrest political authority over our own society and culture from corporations, our own military, and their international allies. If these are not things which we are willing to accept, if we like the life that corporate culture, international capital, and the military class provide for us, we must be willing to accept as the price for these privileges the understanding that a significant percentage of the rest of the world will see us as something ranging from Great Satan to imperialist. (I know, it's not much of a range.) We will also have the periodic obligation of dropping bombs, killing a few civilians in the process, and "accidentally" destroying the occasional pharmaceutical lab in places such as the Sudan, thus obliging our political leaders to behave like state terrorists. And we will still need to send our own soldiers off to fight and die in international police incidents in the name of the preservation of these privileges. But it is a *sacred* lifestyle!

I think it's pretty clear that our *de facto* decision has been for the second option, although that decision has been "unconscious"—that is, not accessible to responsible ethical reason.[4] But even, as I say, if we could imagine bringing these issues successfully to consciousness, if we could oblige truth to stand before the threat of real consequences, my fear is that the choice would be, "I accept the premises of Pure War. I understand that the maintenance of my privilege is dependent on others' misery, and I'm willing to suffer the occasional terrorist attack and consequent military policing to maintain it. And I'm willing that in the name of Homeland Security a dominant part of civilian life be war in the form of an eternal declaration of our willingness to make war."

It is in this sense that we are already, as Virilio puts it, "citizen soldiers." The success of the techno-military is in the fact that people don't recognize their own militarization. Our commitment to technological rationality as "progress" is in reality a commitment to the techno-military as fate. Coming to consciousness about these matters isn't an uncommon thing; in fact, it's so common and banal that we hardly recognize it for what it is. For example, I recently had the following experience. My printer wouldn't work. Why? After a certain period of time, a computer chip on the ink cartridge essentially declared that it was done, never mind that I probably hadn't used a tenth of the ink. So I went to the damned store and paid twenty-five bucks

---

[4] This absence of ethical reason on our end is not lost on Osama bin Laden, who argues in his November 2002 audiotape, "Until when would killing and destruction . . . be our share, while security, stability and happiness are yours? This is unfair, and it is high time that we stand on equal ground. As you kill, you will be killed, as you bomb, you will be bombed." Ariel Sharon couldn't have said it better. In the face of bin Laden's forceful if murderous reason, what does our standard rationale for involvement in the region—"national economic and security interests"—look like, especially to Muslims? It looks like what it is, naked self-interest.

for a new cartridge, took the old one out, replaced it with the new—and, of course, it didn't work. So, I removed the new cartridge and inspected it for God knows what and replaced the culprit to no visible benefit. Driven to the owner's manual, I discovered the unpalatable fact that there were buttons I had to push in a certain sequence before installing the cartridge. I also learned that if I removed the cartridge for inspection, well, that permanently deactivated the clever little piece of crap.

At that point it became luminously clear to me that this machine was training me. And so I concluded by thinking, "What habits of mind are required in order to live in accord with my car, my television, and my computer? And are these new habits of mind good or bad things? And just when do we get to ask these questions?"

This example is perhaps no more significant than the familiar whining about setting the clock on the VCR. But for me it is a sign of a certain resentment in the species about the indignity of having to adapt to the needs of machines. When Virilio looks at similar misadventures, the response he has is that to live a life substantially mediated by technology of one sort or another is to live in a world that has no endurance, that is always "disappearing." The images on the TV do not linger; they disappear. The world outside your car window does not linger; it vanishes. It is the opposite of what Buddhists call "meditative equipoise." One does not live in the moment; one is always being slung into a constantly accelerating future. Faster is better, we think, just as every military general since time immemorial has thought. Velocity is the common term between quotidian life and the logic of military need. (As Lycos founder Bob Davis puts it in the title of his recent book, *Speed Is Life.*)

Back to Virilio:

> Either we wait for the coming of a hypothetical universal state
> with I don't know what primate at its head, or else we finally
> understand that what is at the center is no longer a monarch
> . . . but an absolute weapon. (46)

Osama bin Laden's position is beyond politics. Al-Qaeda is not represented by any state that could articulate its point of view. Al-Qaeda is utterly deterritorialized. It may have temporary hosts, but it doesn't have a home. In this sense, Bush's insistence that there can be no negotiation with terrorism is both redundant and irrelevant. Bin Laden's first premise is that his efforts are post-political and thus outside of any framework for negotiation. What makes this situation doubly ironic is the fact that the United States and its primary trading partners (Canada and Mexico), in lockstep with the purposes of the newly formed European Union, are also engaged in making nation-states irrelevant and antique. Terrorism's deterritorialization is a negative reflection of our own economic and political tendencies. And yet politicians and the media (especially Hollywood) continue to appeal to a sentimental patriotism in order to purchase the consent for our military excursions. The United States may be part of a postmodern global reality without economic or political borders, but its citizens continue to need to be appealed to in more old-fashioned ways.

Equally revealing, if also horrifying, is the manner in which terrorism has seized upon our own technology as its weapons of choice. Our airliners are bombs. Our buildings are bombs. Our nuclear reactors are certainly dirty bombs, *in potentia*, as we've long known. Our bureaucracies (like the postal system) are bombs. And our bombs are their bombs, because every bomb we drop, they believe, ultimately furthers their interests. Even the anthrax they employ was developed by our scientists in our own biological weapons programs. In short, terrorism has seized upon the "accidents" (plane crashes, slaughter on the freeways, nuclear meltdowns, misplaced or stolen anthrax, plutonium, nuclear secrets, etc.) that have always slumbered within technological rationality.[5]

---

[5] One has to wonder how Islamicists explain to themselves their dependence on the technology that is the large part of what they object to in Western culture. Are these methods not self-contaminating for them?

This curious fact should have been made clear on November 12, 2001, when an American Airlines jet headed for the Dominican Republic crashed in Queens. But of course the American media couldn't see it this way without jeopardizing the confidence game it administers. An absolute distinction had to be maintained between terrorist acts of war and a mechanical accident. While the media found it reasonable that Americans should shy away from jets if the reason was that terrorists might be plunging them into buildings, the idea that we should shy away from jets because they have always had a tendency to plunge to the ground in a statistically predictable manner has not been depicted by the media as at all reasonable. On the contrary, such accidents have been managed in the media through expressions of faith in the calculations of actuarial science and cost/benefit analyses, and by faith in the raw ideology of technical progress.

This faith must be maintained in the face of the fact that 42,000 citizens of the United States die annually in traffic accidents, never mind the hundreds of thousands who are injured. According to the U.S. National Traffic Safety Administration, between 1985 and 1999, 3,236,000 people were killed or injured in traffic accidents in the United States. Every ten years we wipe out the population of four cities the size of the one in which I live, Bloomington-Normal, Illinois. Dead. And we leave a population the equivalent of a major metropolitan area (close to three million) as walking wounded, carting around the pain of pins in their ankles, knees like pudding, and ruptured vertebrae. Where is the memorial to those deaths and wounds? How many millions of human beings lost on the roadside over the last century? These numbers dwarf the losses in wars like Vietnam and Korea, and yet they are the result of a "rationalizing" of our communities and our lives. (This does not even begin to consider the *animal* "road kill," a holocaust if there ever was one. Little does our species care.)

How are these deaths represented by the media and the government to national consciousness? Accidents. Statistics. The only clues to the reality of our situation are the chilling little primitive shrines set up by grieving families with white crosses and plastic flowers at the local Dead

Man's Curve, where drunken teenagers immemorial have gone to die. And yet every day we join the march of commuters caught in the same sad and strange necessity of "rush hour," and knowingly we roll the dice.[6]

If we were to construct a national memorial to these automated deaths, I would suggest a mural depicting the opening scene from Jean-Luc Godard's *Weekend*: first, the irrelevant beauty of the French countryside, then the endless highway backed up for miles with motionless but belligerently honking cars, next the bizarre humans caught in the traffic, screaming or playing cards, and finally, at its end, the pathetic and anticlimactic bodies strewn by the bloody roadside.

The "cure" for this "epidemic" is simple: design communities so that people are not obliged to get in cars and drive in maniacal conditions on freeways in order to live. And yet a call for a solution which denies that there is a social good in "commuting" as a national lifestyle would be depicted by media pundits as irrational, just as any "travel anxiety" generated by Queens 11-12 is irrational. The crash in Queens was an "unfortunate coincidence" and is lamented largely because it is yet another psychological impediment to the much-desired recovery of the economy. So what can you do to help your country? Bury your silly fears. Fly somewhere. Better yet, fly somewhere and go shopping. And that frisking at the gate? Enjoy!

---

[6] International statistics regarding automobile-related fatalities are utterly dismaying. According to Adnan Hyder of the Johns Hopkins Bloomberg School of Public Health, in 1998 there were an estimated 1,170,694 deaths caused by road traffic worldwide. Worse yet, for every driver killed in an accident, two pedestrians were killed. Twenty-five percent of the world's hospital beds are occupied by road accident survivors. Traffic injuries are the second leading cause of ill health and premature death worldwide for people ages fifteen through forty-four, second only to HIV/AIDS. The projection is that by 2020 road deaths will not decrease, but they will nonetheless be overtaken as a leading cause of death in the world by heart disease, which gallops apace because of the growing popularity of high-fat Western foods (i.e., hamburgers and french fries) and American cigarettes, both of which, of course, are romanticized and endorsed by exported Hollywood entertainment. So much for the manna of the exportation of Western lifestyle and technology. No wonder economic globalization is so fiercely opposed by many European countries. It's no secret to them that our exports mean their deaths.

What bin Laden seems to understand is that Pure War, understood as the techno-militarization of the human world, can be pushed where it has been headed all along but where perhaps it would rather not go on someone else's command: techno-military apocalypse. In this sense, his destination is not all that different from the anticipation of our own fundamentalist Baptists: the End of Days. Revelation. The Antichrist. The Second Coming. This is the conclusion of the confrontation between the Holy Warrior and the Global State Technician. Unlike the gruesome Cold War relationship between the nuclear couple, the United States and the Soviet Union, in which deterrence provided the Peace of Pure War (the peace of the "balance of terror," or "mutually assured mass destruction"), our new antagonist has no illusions about that grim dance. Muslims of bin Laden's stripe will have the life they imagine (however cruel and medieval) or they will have death, about which they have no fear or illusions because the religious thinking at the heart of their activities makes death irrelevant.

It's hard to imagine anything gloomier than this analysis. Fortunately, Virilio does offer an alternative and a way of confronting the present madness, but it is a strategy of resistance that is addressed not only to the Taliban but also to our own techno-military state. What he offers is this: a pacifism that works religiously in that it returns us to our "identity as mortal beings." (79)

One of the most revealing news clips I've heard since September 11 was an analysis of "consumer confidence" which pointed out that one of the hindrances to a return to normal by American consumers was precisely that the destruction and death involved in the World Trade Center had turned people away from the superficial happiness of consumption and had made them all too aware of their human vulnerability.[7] The destruction of the World Trade Center turned people

---

[7]As I revised this section in the summer of 2002, roughly nine months after 9-11, the local newspaper reported that July had been a record month for births in our town. Apparently, here in Normal, after the WTC tragedy, folks had turned in all seriousness to "human things" for a moment at least.

toward marriage, church, and commitment to others, according to news reports. Something like that turn, oddly enough, could be what Virilio sees as the beginning of the internal dissolution of the empire of Pure War and the religious fanaticism it has empowered. The Soviet Union was not confronted and defeated; it was dissolved internally by its failure to provide for the human needs of its own citizens (and I'm not talking about the need for television sets and satellite hookups). Perhaps it is a similar spiritual turn (stripped of its heteronormativity, I hope) that can confront the dominance of the military, the technocrats, and multinational capital in the New World Order.

2.

It's important to add, before continuing this journey, that Virilio's vision is not an entirely new story. In fact, it is the oldest story of modernity. In the work of thinkers like Theodor Adorno and the Frankfurt School of critical inquiry, it is the story of Good Enlightenment (emancipation, human self-realization, creativity, and democracy) versus Bad Enlightenment (instrumental rationality and the logic of efficiency, profit, performance, and cost/benefit analysis). In a book that we seem to have unhappily forgotten, Theodore Roszak's *The Making of a Counter Culture* (1969), the argument is explicit and very much still to the point. Roszak's antagonist was what he called "technocracy":

> For our purposes here it will be enough to define the technocracy as that society in which those who govern justify themselves by appeal to technical experts who, in turn, justify themselves by appeal to scientific forms of knowledge. And beyond the authority of science, there is no appeal. (8)

Roszak speaks, as does Virilio, of a dance macabre between capitalism, technology, and militarism:

We call it "education," the "life of the mind," the "pursuit of the truth." But it is a matter of machine-tooling the young to the needs of our various baroque bureaucracies: corporate, governmental, military, trade union, educational.

We call it "free enterprise." But it is a vastly restrictive system of oligopolistic market manipulation, tied by institutionalized corruption to the greatest munitions boondoggle in history and dedicated to infantilizing the public by turning it into a herd of compulsive consumers. (16)

In the wake of the Enron scandal, our high-tech War Against Terror, and George II's Consumer Patriotism, it is not possible for me to say that Roszak's description is outdated.

What is, of course, outdated is his optimism that the resistance of youth culture in the sixties had a long future ahead of it:

It is still a small, if boisterous minority of the young who now define the generational conflict. But the conflict will not vanish when those who are now twenty reach thirty; it may only reach its peak when those who are now eleven and twelve reach their late twenties. (Say, about 1984.) We then may discover that what a mere handful of beatniks pioneered in Allen Ginsberg's youth will have become the life style of millions of college-age young. (40)

I don't need to remind you that by 1984 we were in the middle of the Reagan-Bush years during which the generation of the sixties and those eleven-year-olds of whom Roszak speaks so hopefully were far from "turned on." They were "plugged in." The day of the personal computer, cell phone, and Sharper Image was just dawning. If the counterculture had hoped to turn work into life, just the opposite was happening. Now we work at home and in the car. We work while walking down the street, cell phone applied to ear. With the advent of Web TV, even the TV has been made potentially part of our jobs. And so our very living rooms are workstations. The private is colonized by work and the demand for obeisance to work.

Yeah, but Jerry Rubin on Wall Street? For the counterculture, Rubin's defection had the finality if not the drama of the fall of the Berlin Wall. I hope he lost his shirt in the NASDAQ debacle, the scapegrace.

In turning to a consideration of the technological imagination, I am suggesting not only that it is the real moving force in the political imagination; I am also suggesting that it is the moving force behind *all* expressions of the American imagination. The mass media is utterly and inescapably technologized, and it creates an appropriate reverence for technology in its products. Technology is the God that worships itself. Even the field of the humanities now imagines itself through a dense, mechanical jargon that, if you could drop it, would go "clank." This is to say nothing of the resources that are being poured into the creation of distance education and the aura of the inevitability of what distance education theorist Mark Taylor calls "network culture."

In the arena of the technological, there is nothing impoverished about the American imagination. So powerful have the assumptions of national technophilia become that they have achieved the self-evidence of nature. Technology is our nature. The first socializing experiences for our children are now with televisions and computer games. They learn through machines not only how to be members of a particular culture but also how to be human. There is nothing innocent or innocuous about those bizarre shmoos that we call Teletubbies. (I don't care if one of them is gay; they're a public menace.) In short, it is no longer the case that machines are an extension of our needs. On the contrary, we are extensions of the imperatives of machines. Virtual afterthoughts. Like domesticated dogs (who have over the eons evolved childlike facial expressions that prompt humans to care for them), humans have morphed in an obliging way to seem more efficient and capable, more machine-like, in the photoreceptive eyes of our machines, as if we feared being abandoned by them. It has reached a point where to be technophobic (or simply technically maladroit) is not to risk mere irrelevance or incompetence; it is to risk isolation. The community of man now sits at personalized consoles, whether in office cubicles or in the living room. It is here that we have our famous Global Village. Our fateful paradox: to live in this community, you have to be alone.

We can think of the technological imagination in at least two ways. First, it is the more innocent process of invention. This silicon chip, this electronic pulse, this synthetic diaphragm, this sensor, this vacuum tube, this gadget or gizmo that we've chanced upon—what can it do for us in what context? Can it amuse us? Feed us? Cure us? Propel us? Can it induce the feeling of religious ecstasy? Can it run an operation that used to require the employment of twenty tribal boys? Can it help us to fool our computers into thinking we're like them? This is the technological imagination as invention.

But this invention always happens in a context. Our context is in substantial part global corporations and militarism. In our culture at present, the technological imagination invents for that amorphous thing that we really know not at all, "the economy." But first it invents for the military.

The reason that the technological imagination has these particular masters has to do with a second form of the technological imagination that borders on the social imagination more broadly construed. The problem that this second form seeks to address is this: What stories shall we tell ourselves about the "good" of technology for our culture? This work of the imagination is hybrid. In part, it is about describing and justifying the "good," and in part it is about explaining, apologizing for, or condemning technology's relationship to that "good." The American imagination is not impoverished in this respect. Rather, it is feverish. It is as if we were in a slow-motion disaster dream and we wanted to bring just enough day-lit consciousness to the situation so that it could both make sense and stop. There is a certain species desperation in the invention of this narrative.

What I'd like to do is look at a range of efforts to imagine the role of technology in our world, beginning with what strike me as the most malign and dangerous narratives and proceeding toward more utopic suggestions. I say *utopic* because I believe that finally the only thing that can save us from our technologies, and from thinking of ourselves as extensions of those technologies, is the imagination intervening, subverting, derailing the disaster machine with a forceful counter-imagination, counter-discourse, and, of course and necessarily, counterculture. This work of the counter-imagination will include, I urgently insist, technologies, including computers. But our understanding of their social standing will be utterly transformed. This will require, first, that we come to understand our present relationship to technology as a "disaster." No more illusions on that score.

Some of you might like me to justify my use of the word "disaster," holding hopefully, as many do, to the illusion that we have "better living" through our machines. Well, to begin with, this disaster is no secret and needs no explanation to the two-thirds of the world that has been the beneficiary of the technological manna we or our clients have dropped in the form of bombs (Israelis on Palestinians, Iraqis on Kurds, etc.). Nor is it a secret to the millions of people in Asia that our computer-driven finance industry helped to impoverish in the late nineties. Nor is the disaster obscure in any way for conservative Muslims, who have tried to tell us in the clearest way they can that our entertainment industry is a disaster for their understanding of Islam. To which our blunt reply has always been, "Change." Or else. Put these three forms of disaster together in one place, as we have in the Middle East, add to it good old-fashioned imperial exploitation of natural resources (oil), and you have something that I think it's fair to call a smoothly functioning disaster.

These disasters-for-others have "blown back" on our own shores, and we are now obliged to live in persistent anxiety about what will blow back next. It is a reasonable anxiety. How hard is it, after all, to imagine one damaged Muslim with, in one hand, a bit of plutonium or weapons-grade uranium the size of a baseball, and, in the other hand, one stick of dynamite, standing at, oh, say, Madison and Fifty-fifth Street in midtown Manhattan?[8] How hard is that to imagine? And what happens to our vaunted American-style capitalist juggernaut if this is done simultaneously in Manhattan, Washington, D.C., and Hollywood? In response to which threat our political leaders, playing a game of last-man-standing, suggest that we bomb the hell out of them first. Bomb Iraq because it might have weapons we surely have and surely use wherever we think they're needed. Even if they do have weapons, it's because we gave them to the Iraqis in the first place. Oh, *buena idea*, you stalwart men. You have just recreated Mickey Mouse's nightmare in the "Sorcerer's Apprentice" sequence of *Fantasia*. Mickey couldn't defeat the brooms by whacking them, and we won't defeat resistance to global capitalism, militarism, and Hollywood by dropping bombs. Now everyone in Iraq thinks, "What the hell is the difference if I blow myself up or wait till they blow me up? I'm gonna take some consumer capitalists [a.k.a. infidels] with me."

Or, less apocalyptically (I think), what does the following fact mean, if not disaster? The most contaminated food source on the planet is human breast milk. According to Sandra Steingraber in her book *Having Faith* (2001),

When it comes to persistent organic pollutants (POPs), breast milk is the most contaminated of all human foods. It typically carries concentrations of organochlorine pollutants that are ten to twenty times higher than those in cow's milk. Indeed, prevailing levels of chemical contaminants in human milk often exceed legally allowable limits in commercial foodstuffs. One leading researcher concluded in 1996, "Breast milk, if regulated like infant formula, would commonly violate Food

---

[8] The Pentagon is currently (and very seriously) studying a proposal to create a "wall" of high-tech devices around major American cities to detect nuclear bombs and radioactive dirty bombs coming in by car, truck, or boat. This is a Star Wars defense system on the interstate.

and Drug Administration action levels for poisonous or delete-
rious substances in food and could not be sold." (251)

I call that an everyday disaster passing for the good life.

Having staked my claim for the American military-industrial-
technocratic empire as disaster machine, let me proceed to some of
the particulars of the work of the imagination in relation to technology. The first scenario is from what I'll call the Adolescent Abyss, a
conceptual place where the monomania for technology renders all
other considerations not so much irrelevant as boring. Social considerations of justice barely exist, so enthralled are we here by the
prospect of bombs going off, enemies being crushed, in a matrix requiring at least three of the following in any one incident: satellites in
geosynchronous orbit (for the techno-geek looking at the world from
the depth of the Adolescent Abyss, our victory in space is, if not more
important, certainly more "awesome" than our victory in the Cold
War), unmanned air vehicles, sensors of all kinds, gunships, the
Global Positioning System, laser guidance systems, and nuclear missile interceptors (space-based lasers are a big fave [actually, space-
based *anything* is a big fave (actually actually, just the notion of being
"space-based," the mere sound of the hyphenated word, its quick-
rhyme poetry, rocks this mind like a jolt of acid)]).

    In an essay titled "Peace Is War" that eerily echoes one of Virilio's
themes, Bruce Sterling, science fiction writer and proto-cyber punker,
considers "the new frontier of missile defense, where peacekeeping
space lasers battle a storm of rogue nukes." ("Peace Is War," *Wired,* April
2002) Sterling seems to have intuited the substance of Virilio's concept
of Pure War in his idea that peace is war, but he has a very different reading of its political and ethical meaning. The idea that peace must be
based on the eternal readiness to make war is for Sterling just a way of
saying that the United States should use its global military preemi-
nence to enforce a *pax Americana.* The United States must become As-
trocop. It's a dirty job in a dangerous world, but someone's got to do it.

Our destiny as global cop occurs to Sterling with the sort of trite, battlefield-Europe machismo that used to underlie the political assumptions of magazines like *True*. Back in the 1950s, *True* was the only magazine that my WWII vet father subscribed to. Its repeated stories of brave GIs making the world safe for American-style democracy was the beginning of the mythology of the U.S. as universal enforcer of the true and the free. The rhetoric, frankly, hasn't gotten much subtler, even if the scientific pretensions have. We're peacekeepers. They're rogues and lunatics. They threaten world peace with their mad plans, those Iraqis and North Koreans. We bravely step forward with our superior capabilities to make sure that they fail.

This threadbare scenario is convincing enough to the mind in the Adolescent Abyss. It is just sufficient to move this mind to the next moment, the pornography of technophilia, virtually oozing with acronyms (MILSTAR, DMJP, GPS) and the orgasmic certainty that something or somebody somewhere is going to get good and blowed-up. It is as if this were really some sort of sex cult. What more could a geeky kinda guy want? Girls? Fah! Get that *Playboy* shit outta my face. Gimme the real juice. Gimme the Global Positioning coordinates, now the laser-guided cruise missile, now stand the fuck back.

For this mind the idea that we can "strike any spot on Earth at will," as Sterling writes, is such a *good* thing.[9]

Sterling's representation of technophilia's Adolescent Abyss is not only violent; it is also haughty and disdainful of others. "The alternative to destroying Washington," he writes, "is clear: world peace, Washington-style . . . no war as war is usually understood. No Sommes, no

---

[9] Let me suggest a little experiment to you. Take a copy of the Sierra Club's *Sierra* magazine in one hand and a copy of *Wired* in the other. Go someplace quiet and read the two at the same time. Now you have the substance of a real Culture War. It has nothing to do with C. P. Snow's "two cultures," and it has nothing to do with postmodern tenured radicals. Both magazines are utterly dependent upon science. But the narrative trajectories of their social imaginations are wildly different. Do trees even exist for *Wired*?

Verduns, or Iwo Jima, probably not even any Vietnams or Afghanistans. Just Space War IV, V, VI, until everyone gets it, the last stiff-necked mountain tribe, the last hermit kingdom." The Bible describes the Jews as "stiff-necked" as a way of indicating the justice of God's actions when he "smites" them. According to the Bible, the stiff-necked Jews got what they deserved. In Sterling's view, our competitors, on the other side of American might, also live on sufferance. They live only to die if we will it. For we imagine ourselves in the place, as Dante said of God, "where willing and doing are one."

Sterling closes his essay by considering the new "genuine ruling class" of technocrats, drinking coffee in Beltway Starbucks. They are an "imperial elite," and Sterling couldn't be more smug about his (and our) vicarious triumph through them.

> Washington's war wonks don't seem actively oppressive, bloody-handed, or evil. Old Glory hangs all over town in its riveted incarnation as the 9-11 battle flag, but there are no jackboot parades or martyr cults. Let's face it, the world might do much worse.

But it could also do much better if it had access to a process leading to social justice and universal well-being, not technically enabled well-being stateside at the expense of substantial misery abroad. Sterling's logic seems to be that if we don't look like old-style evil (read: Nazis), we must be good. We are neither good nor evil. We are the soul of ambiguity. We cut both ways and at the same time. Yes, the war wonks at Starbucks are clean. Sterile as scalpels all lined up.

3.

And how do the leaders of the new Information Economy, the titans of e.commerce, narrate our future? What's their social imaginary? What do they think?

Not much, as it turns out.

Really.

Not much.

Take, for example, Lycos CEO Bob Davis's *Speed Is Life* (2001). Lycos, along with Yahoo!, was one of the first Web portals to achieve "brand recognition," and with it millions in startup investments. In a six-year period, under Davis's leadership, the company grew from $2 million to $5.4 billion in value. In 2000, it was the linchpin in the formation of a multinational company, Terralycos, made up of media giants Bertelsmann (Germany) and Telefónica (Spain).

I imagined, before reading Davis's book, that he would be a sort of visionary, seeing the far-reaching importance and implications of the Net in a way others couldn't. Hence his phenomenal success. And, in fact, *Speed Is Life* begins with some startling claims, all of which confirm Virilio's contentions about the military, speed, and technology. Davis begins his book in this way:

> Not long ago, I was invited to tour a number of U.S. military facilities as a guest of William Cohen, then Secretary of Defense. The purpose of my visits was to gain firsthand knowledge of how the armed forces use technology to improve combat readiness. . . . I saw how much our military personnel cherish [cherish?—a curious word choice] speed—and the technology that delivers it. They believe that the United States is able to gather, analyze, distribute, and act on information faster than any other country on earth. Our military superiority, they told me, derives in large measure from our ability to unleash an information blitzkrieg. . . . [An even curiouser choice of words. Are we being told here that our military "cherishes" its ability to make war like Nazis? The oxymoron is shocking: a tender brutality.](15)

Clearly, Virilio, Sterling, and Davis are seeing the same things, even if they come to wildly different conclusions about what these things mean. Davis sees the extension of military speed in business and everyday life. Speed is the great differentiator. It is an essential survival tool. But of course "speed" is a relative term. Fast today is slow tomorrow. The critical term (and it is Virilio's term as well) is "acceleration." As Davis notes, "We live in a world where a company is measured by its ability to accelerate everything from manufacturing to marketing, from hiring to distributing." (17)

The utopic destination of this logic is "instantaneity." Davis again: "Technology has taken us into a whole new dimension of time, what some call Internet time. It comes in three speeds: fast, faster, and instant, which means *right now*." (18) We know what it means, Bob. The question is how this utopia is distinguishable from our apocalypse when it is applied to the logistics of warfare. There is no room for diplomacy, negotiation, or "fail safe" in a war run by computers programmed to instantaneity.[10] That reality is a not inconsequential part of Davis's vaunted high-tech business paradigm.

Do you recall Superman's evil antithesis, Bizarro? Where Superman was all clean, tan, and rounded lines, Bizarro was icy-pale, with a spiky haircut (which would now be quite fashionable among the young) and angular lines. It was almost as if Bizarro had been carved with a large chisel from a block of ice. Well, Davis is a sort of Bizarro-Buddha. He is the Buddha negated. If the Buddha is about mindfulness and being in the moment, Bizarro-Buddha-Davis is about fleeing into the next moment. Says Bizarro-Buddha: "To act fast is to live fully." (33)

---

[10] This tension is bad enough as it stands: it makes *Dr. Strangelove*'s twenty minutes to nuclear winter seem like an eternity. The gap is presently three minutes. Dr. Helen Caldicott of Physicians for Social Responsibility describes an event on January 25, 1995, in which "Russia detected signals from an American missile that had just been launched off the coast of Norway carrying a U.S. scientific probe." (11) The Russians assumed they were being attacked. "For the first time in history, the Russian computer containing nuclear launch codes was opened." (11) Boris Yeltsin had three minutes to make a decision. Fortunately, during that interval, the missile veered away from Russia.

If Buddha was about no ego, Bizarro-Buddha is about getting "attention" (which he means in exactly the way mothers mean it when they speak of three-year-olds "needing attention"). Davis says of personal Web sites: "The reason they built the sites was simple and primal—we all want attention, recognition, and a forum in which to share our accomplishments." (25) What the Buddha calls a delusion, Bizarro-Buddha calls "primal."

If the Buddha is about the futility of grasping at the material world, trying to hold what can't be held, Bizarro-Buddha has a different philosophy, which he calls, "If you let up, you lose." In short, Davis advocates grasping. Grasp like hell. Hold on tight to the sucker. Given Bizarro-Buddha's commitment to speed, a little white-knuckled holding on is understandable.

Bizarro-Buddha even has some koan-like gems for contemplation while holding on and being flung at the speed of instantaneity into our utopic/apocalyptic future. For instance:

> Adaptability makes the difference between complacency and conquest. (24)

Ponder that, Little Grasshopper. Or:

> Half the world's inhabitants have never made a phone call, yet Internet traffic doubles every 100 days.

Hmmm. It's not "Why has Bodhidharma left for the East?" but it will do for our enduring faith in technology as destiny.

Of course, we might say that these koans are just problems in logic that a decent copy editor could clear up, but the success of Davis and Lycos was not dependent on subtle logic or even plain old logical logic. It was dependent on really shopworn logic. Finally, Davis is not Bizarro-Buddha, and he is not the visionary philosopher-entrepreneur of the Internet. He is an American businessman, and he thinks the things that American businessmen have thought for generations. You can know how Davis thinks any day of the week through a quick visit to the local Rotary Club. For the bulk of his book, Davis demonstrates

that the road to victory (his word) in the new commercial frontier of
e.commerce is through:

- hard work and sacrifice

- "dogged determination" (also "relentless determination")

- wanting to be number one

- getting big fast

- putting the customer first

- creating brand recognition

- creating loyalty among employees by treating them well

- remembering that companies are about *profits*

I had always heard that businesspeople thought such things, but
these seemed such clichéd truisms that I said, "Nah, they don't *really* think like that, not the new visionary high-tech entrepreneurs
of our future." But here was Lycos insider Bob Davis telling me,
"Oh, yes, we *do* think like that." In the end, Bob Davis's genius is
reducible to this one observation: the Internet is a great place to
advertise. It's like TV with more buttons. It's about commercials.
And so, inevitably, the Web is *all* about commerce. In a Scripps
Howard News Service release dated July 2, 2002, the Federal Trade
Commission warned seven Internet search engines, including
Davis's own Terralycos, that they were required "to fully disclose
that paid advertisements are included in search engine results." In
other words, your searches on the Web are driven by who has paid
to be among the results, and your results are indistinguishable from
advertisements for products. And you *asked* for them! This is the
only "information" this "economy" is finally interested in giving
you.

In any event, I feel now that I can merge with this world in which we imagine ourselves accelerating into the future, grasping as we go, and all of us singing "Quality is job one!" as the G-force smears our lips back in a smile or grimace.

4.

Even though scientists have the most to do with the technological imagination as invention, they generally feel very little responsibility to participate in the technological imagination as part of a larger social imagination. In other words, scientists make little effort to create an idea of a human order in which their creations have a place and which can be argued for as "good" and desirable. As Helen Caldicott describes in her 2002 book *The New Nuclear Danger*, "Scientists have always operated in absolute secrecy, which gave them the anonymity they needed to preserve their work. They used a language that was incomprehensible to all but the most educated, and, like physicians, they hid behind an arcane scientific complexity, never emerging to inform the world what they were doing." (13–14) Thus has it ever been, I suppose.

A conversation I'd like to see (but won't):

Concerned citizen: "So, you've created a virulent new strain of anthrax which has been genetically designed to be resistant to antibiotics and which can be easily and broadly dispersed as a fine powder?"

Scientist: "Yes, I have."

Concerned citizen: "And why was this a beneficial thing to do?"

Scientist: "I work for the United States government here at Fort Detrick, and I was asked to do this by the United States Army."

Concerned citizen: "Yes, but in what way was this a good and desirable thing, to have this virulent strain of genetically manipulated anthrax as a possibility and now a threat in the human world?"

At this point the scientist reveals the essential poverty of his *social* imagination (never mind that his powers of *scientific* imagination are so fertile that he could splice anthrax into salmon and send them swimming up Puget Sound if Seattle were ever to step out of line again). He mumbles something about not being a philosopher, then something really lame about duty, love of country, and national defense. Meanwhile, his snowy death, fine as the powder that you'd pat your baby's butt with, has literally "blown back" on these shores. The anthrax that showed up in envelopes in the halls of Congress, in post offices, and in the junk mail of grannies in New England was our own genetic monster, the product of our own technological imagination. As part of a defense program, there are some obvious bugs in the product, but as a disaster machine, it hits on all cylinders, baby!

Nevertheless, science is not entirely free to do what it wants without the support of a rationale for its social good. It just needs some help with making its case. For this, science has a variety of "explainers" who can translate the meaning and the importance of science's world and the technology that comes from it, and argue for it as a social good. This is done with customary dunce-like aptitude by our political representatives (using the motifs of profit, defense, and "progress"), and it is done in more subtle ways (for that part of the public which is literate enough to care) in books of popular science and—most effectively—in science programs on public TV. On programs provided by the PBS series NOVA, produced by Devillier Donegan Enterprises, and underwritten by the Alfred P. Sloan Foundation, media writers and producers help scientists to "make nice" to the rest of us nonscientists and create a case for the interest and desirability of their work. One recent program, which commands our attention at this point, was called *Beyond Human*, produced by Thomas Lucas in association with PBS and Devillier Donegan. It begins with the following narrative:

> A strange new era is dawning. An era of revolutionary experiments. Wired torsos. Chip implanted brains. Creatures of silicon and steel. Welcome to the age of cyborgs and androids. As

humans become more machine-like, and machines more human, the line between biology and technology is starting to blur. And in the process we may just be reinventing the future of our species.

In this age of advancing technology, we are becoming increasingly impatient with the bodies nature has given us. With our frailties, our failing sight, our broken limbs, the crippling limitations of illness. While our minds soar, our bodies seem frozen in time. What if we could build a better body? Use technology to fix this human form and then actually improve upon it, make it stronger, faster, smarter, create the human of the future today?

This, my friends, is the technological imagination as social imagination. It is hard at work, at last making itself responsible for accounting for the relationship of its work to the human world. Is this science? No. This is science fiction in the most literal sense. It is science's attempt to imagine its world. The power of its efforts will come not from hard evidence, its presentation of scientifically validated Truth, but from its rhetorical and narrative skills, both verbal and visual. But this little narrative is tense with assumptions and claims, none of which can be demonstrated, all of which are contestable. This helps us to see that the role of science fiction as a literary genre has been not only to indulge in technophilia or futurology, but to provide what science never adequately provides on its own: a narrative account of its practices and a critique (in story form) of its assumptions. Kurt Vonnegut's early science fictions, especially *Player Piano* (in which Vonnegut questions the human good of universal automation), are models of the form. Unfortunately, the creators of *Beyond Human* are not artists with Vonnegut's critical eye.

Even a cursory examination of *Beyond Human*'s opening narrative would reveal at least the following issues and problems:

- What do the writers mean by an "era" or an "age"? "A strange new era is dawning": this is pure *Star Trek* stuff; it is the equivalent of a fiction writer's request for "willing suspension of disbelief"—that is, we neither believe nor disbelieve in the idea of "eras," but we'll put aside our skepticism so that the tale can proceed.

- "We"—just what or who is this "we" that the narration assumes? The fiction of a united humanity? Why is it legitimate to so blithely discount the half of the human population that does not benefit from Western technology? "We" are not one in our interests and needs—not by a long shot. Another "willing suspension of disbelief" is required in order to proceed. "We" acquiesce; please proceed, yet again, Mr. Narrator.

- This "we" is said to be "impatient with the bodies nature has given us." In what sense are we "impatient," and what are we to make of the superficial assumption that something called "nature" has "given" us our bodies? Did we remember to say thank you?

- "Our minds soar." What evidence of this does the narrative present? Is the mind soaring in this narrative, or is it limping along on stale sci-fi contrivances and popular science (like the fiction that there's something called nature out there that gives us things); or can the mind be said to soar because of the evidence provided by the remarkable feats of technology? It is most likely the case (sez I) that it is the latter, which makes this argument a very rarefied example of begging the question: to answer the question "Does the technological imagination serve us well?" we first assume that it is "soaring."

- "Our bodies are frozen in time." What can this mean? Our bodies have failed to be as new and improved as the myriad devices the technological imagination has invented? The computing power of computers doubles its capacity every eighteen months, but what does the body have to show for itself? Same old bag of bones, same old mortal failure.

- "What if we could build a better body?" At last we come to the moment of full revelation; this is a fiction, *mon cher*; but it is also a proposition that the narration will need to find a way to argue: the proposition is that it is a good thing to supplement or replace the human body with machines.

We can move now to the body of this documentary argument. In the course of the first hour (part I, "Body Electric"),[11] we are presented with the following realities, in this order.

First, the human body supplemented by technology can be cured of diseases and disabilities. *Beyond Human* personalizes these possibilities by allowing us to meet some of the people who have been helped, like a woman who was injured in a snowboarding accident in which her spinal cord was damaged, rendering her a paraplegic. Surgeons placed a small computer in her abdomen that sends signals to electrodes in her back and legs, stimulating muscle movement. Through practice and therapy, she was able eventually to harness the artificially induced contractions into movement. Eventually she was able to stand and move.

Second, computer technology can (and, according to this documentary, will) lead to chip implants in humans for monitoring health and providing Global Positioning (so that we know where we are at every instant). This tracking is already done with pets and children. Eventually we will all have a little personal database in such a chip so that people outfitted with the appropriate scanners will be able to download our personal bios and read them on a tiny display on their sunglasses. We'll learn things about each other like: "Hi, my name is Mindy! I've been homeless for the last six months (since I lost my job with Our Skin, the synthetic skin company, and my contract for my Livingcubicle™ home along with it), but my Web site is still up and running. I'd like to find a job in Glam-Bod Tech, in research, application, or even meat archiving. Please leave a message

---

[11] Can't you feel that most mortal and elemental and fully embodied of poets, Walt Whitman, turning in his cold nineteenth-century grave? Whitman was happy about electric lights — not robots taking over our bodies!

at gomindygirl@techlife.com if you know of a suitable position for me. Thanks for scanning my implant and thanks for caring!" To which Mr. Scanner responds by thinking, "Hoo boy, another loser. A meat archiver! Walk on by, brother; walk on by." Eventually, according to this narration, we will come to feel vulnerable if we are not constantly monitored and located. This is part of the benefit of living in the emerging "Nano Age," where we can, as *Beyond Human* assures us, "control nature at the atomic level." Or, from a very different perspective, as Marshall McLuhan put it, "The human person who thinks, works, or dreams himself into the role of a machine is as funny an object as the world provides." (100)

Beyond Human next argues that the United States Army is "beginning to embrace" our shared entry into this Nano Age.[12] We are obliged to ignore, once again, the fact that *Beyond Human* has reversed the cause-and-effect logic of the military's involvement. *Beyond Human* would have us believe that this Nano Age is an independent development of civilian science. But it was, of course, the military that drove the first development of the World Wide Web, and Department of Defense grants continue to fund much of the emerging primary research in digital technology.

For instance, the Associated Press reported on June 9, 2002, that the military is putting up $25 million of a $60 million primary research project to teach a computer common sense. A database named Cyc has been fed 1.4 million truths and generalities about daily life so that it can automatically make assumptions humans make. Researchers have even made the database accessible to the public so that the public can add to the mix whatever little nuggets of common sense it has. Never mind that no one anywhere has a clue what the term "common sense" means. A lot of things that pass

---

[12] What in the world is going on here? First, Bob Davis tells us that the military "cherishes" technology; now we're being told that they "embrace" it. What's next? It's horrible to consider. Perhaps we'll be told that technology gets military guys horny. Not to worry. It's just that old odd couple, eros and mechanical death.

for common sense are famously ideological, bigoted, or plain old meanly stupid. Perhaps the hope is that when our decision-making creations are racing along, deciding the future of the race, functioning beyond the realm of human negotiation, making split-second decisions about whether or not that projectile is a nuclear warhead or India's new waste-disposal program sending garbage into outer space, just perhaps it will pause and say, "The country of India would not attack the country of Us. We eat a lot of their Indian-style food. In addition, we have more and bigger bombs of the type nuclear. Therefore, India would be stupid to attack Us. But many of Us think people of the type East Indian are stupid. And if it is a bomb, many of Us think we don't want to look like a weenie." The computer searches its commonsense archive a bit more, unsatisfied with its conclusions to this point, and comes up with this nugget of common wisdom, contributed by citizens in Idaho. "Guns don't kill; people do. Hit first, ask questions later. Make my day. Do you feel lucky, punk? *Hasta la vista*, baby. I love the smell of napalm. I'm not going to hit you. Like hell I'm not." This logic took a nanosecond to concoct. It all makes me yearn for Stanley Kubrick's HAL, the dysfunctional computer. We need more dysfunctional computers and machines of all kinds so that we never forget just how flawed and dangerous they are, and we never make the mistake of assuming that we've built "sense" into them.

In any event, to return to *Beyond Human*'s doggedly optimistic and good-natured narrative, our future wired soldiers will really be something. "The next generation infantryman is a cyborg soldier, a techno-warrior." Each soldier will be part of a wireless field Internet. Each soldier will be chip-implanted. Plugged in. Ready to roll. "For the enemy of the future, death will be digital."

They make it sound so optimistic. Death for them. Toys for us. But I hope that none of our present enemies, imagining themselves as future enemies, watch PBS. A little line like "Your death will be digital" could really hurt their feelings. Or piss them off. "Oh, my death will be digital, infidel? Well, here's what *your* death will be like." The imagined audience for these programs is really only upper-middle-class North Americans, isn't it? No one else in the world watches TV. Right?

Next, we turn to commerce. "The revolution is being sold, hard," *Beyond Human* tells us. In the commercial world, the body is merely a platform for techno-fashion. Implanted databases, monitors, and accessories are "this year's hot items for the fashion forward." Soon, we will be wearing the Internet like a necklace. One of the mavens of the new techno-fashion industry is Katrina Barillova of Charmed, Inc., a former Eastern European intelligence operative. The KGB is the Ralph Lauren of the twenty-first century. And yet, according to sci-fi writer David Brin, if we "cautiously embrace" these new personal technologies, we will be returned to "the old village our ancestors lived in."

Excuse me. I know I have pledged suspended disbelief to this narrative, and I'm trying to be a good sport about it, but incredulity asks for a moment in which to say its piece. Incredulity says, "What 'old village' are you referring to? And why do you imagine that the idea of returning there cozens anyone into accepting your future? Is this village of which you speak so fondly in the Carpathian Mountains? Where are those mountains? In Carpathia? Is the village surrounded by rich forests and colorful songbirds? Is it like the cottage in *Snow White and the Seven Dwarves?* Or is it perchance in good old Missouri? Will we be gathering around the cracker barrel to listen to the androids indulge their homespun humor and tales of yesteryear down at the general sim-store? Will we eat the crackers, or will they be made of silicon? Will we later meet down by the river? Will Reverend Automaton bless us and dunk us in the eternal waters of the Ether Domain? Will the fragrance of genetically modified apple pie drift from matrix to matrix, causing a pang, a yearning, a hankering for the olden times when some of us had tatters of flesh attached to the hydraulics? And will we also have village idiots like in the old days? Because I have a few candidates for you."

Here's how this cant about the emerging interconnected Global

Village of the future is functioning right now. According to an article by David Diamond in the June 2002 issue of *Wired*, the Philippines presently exports 10 percent of its labor to other countries around the world, principally to the United States and Saudi Arabia, but to more than one hundred and fifty foreign countries in all. These workers send back over $6 billion annually. To stay connected to their families, they also send back over one hundred million cell-phone text messages each day. "I miss you; do your homework; send money." But even *Wired* can't help but notice that there's a downside:

> "The social costs of overseas work," says Rosalinda Baldoz of the government's labor registry, "are marital breakup and dropout children who get into drugs or crime. . . ." Aside from separating families, the overseas employment system is also rife with corruption. According to Baldoz, last year the [labor registry] received 2,000 recruitment violations cases for such infractions as overcharging, sneaking workers out with faked visas, and sending them to jobs that never materialized. . . . Often a new contract, written in a foreign language, is forced on the employee once she's in hock for her [recruitment] fees and far away from home.

In short, the primary problem with *Beyond Human*'s presentation of the Global Village is that it is utterly without a global political context. It is only about the privileged First World (minus its own disenfranchised poor). To Filipino workers, the new Global Village looks an awful lot like the old Boss in a Global Company Town. Another day older and deeper in debt. Exploitation. It's reassuring to know that some old values will remain with us in the Global Village of the future.

Think these are all Third World problems? In the August 4, 2002, edition of the *Chicago Tribune*, Walter F. Roche Jr. reported that the McDonald's restaurant chain had recruited students from Poland to work in the United States with the claim that they would make "more money than you could imagine."

But [Peter] Kasprezyk could not buy an item from the dollar menu with his first paycheck. It was zero.

That's because he and four fellow students were docked for $2,000 monthly rent on a two bedroom apartment they share in Abingdon that normally goes for $750 a month. That deduction wiped out every cent Kasprezyk made flipping hamburgers for $8 an hour at a McDonald's outlet.

As with the Filipino workers, the Poles signed a contract in a language they didn't understand.[13]

In the second hour of *Beyond Human*, "Living Machines," we are introduced to the next consequence of science's work in the relationship between humans and machines. Machines become more human:

Imagine a day when machines walk among us. Expressing thoughts, emotions. Demanding their rights. Today, we are breeding intelligence, perhaps even life, into creatures of silicon and steel. A whole new breed of robots is on the rise. And the line between man and machine is starting to blur.

We begin, once again, with accounts of how robot creatures can save human lives: machines that can rescue people from fires. They can also provide us with services like housecleaning and childcare. They can do the work (as they presently are in factories around the

---

[13] In a short program on the growth of the new capitalist economy in Romania, presented on PBS's *Frontline* the week of October 28, 2002, Andrei Codrescu revealed that one source of new capital for Romania is the training and exporting of young girls to Japan to serve as geishas. According to the Romanian entrepreneur in charge of this export business, the girls are all patriotic and will return to Romania to invest in their country. Without doubt, they too will take cell phones with them for the purpose of keeping in touch with Mom and Dad. It's all part of the great new information economy working among virtual states. A world without borders. Unlimited possibility. One has to wonder what Charles Dickens would have made of it all. Great expectations. Bleak house, indeed.

world) that humans don't want to do. And there's nothing exceptional, according to our PBS program, about these new machines acting in the place of humans, because for centuries humans have tried to reproduce themselves mechanically. We're just getting very good at it now.

The New Robotics produces creatures of real intelligence, which means they can not only be programmed; they can also gather experience, learn from it, and change their actions based upon what they've learned. Not only are they intelligent; they are also expressive. Tiny cameras in the eyes of the robots recognize human expressions and react accordingly. They can even blush. With these lifelike 'bots "we can't help but be drawn in." Ultimately, the New Robotics may not create humans, but it will create "persons" with legal rights and a full capacity to interact with humans.

Here, folks, is a new discrimination, a distinction without a difference, between "humans" and "persons." Huh? I suspect we'll come to enjoy this distinction about as much as we've enjoyed the idea that corporations have legal standing as individuals and a constitutionally guaranteed right to free speech that overwhelms any speech an actual human individual could utter.

"The day of the humanoid is coming soon." For the producers of *Beyond Human*, this is an inevitable and, in the absence of reasons to the contrary, probably a desirable destiny. The only negative imagined within this work is the Frankenstein scenario in which our robots go autonomous and turn on us, as in the *Terminator* movies. This is the action/adventure version of a scenario in which, through superior intelligence and adaptive capacities, the robots out-evolve us. But Hans Moravec, of Carnegie Mellon University's robotics program, is "not too bothered" by this possibility. Not to worry, he says, because the robots are like our children! "The robots will survive, and the robots are our offspring." I don't think he imagines that the use of the word "offspring" is loose or metaphoric; in fact, it is an interesting word choice, engaging the mechanics of springs as it does. *Boing!* "In the long run," he adds, "that's the way it's going to be anyway."

In the April 2000 issue of *Wired*, Sun Microsystems founder Bill Joy echoes this sentiment in an article titled "Why the Future Doesn't Need Us." Joy gives the human race thirty years to come to terms with its own cybernetic creations. Or else.

There is an awful lot to say about the way *Beyond Human* renders our future. We could jump feet first into the ethico-religious middle of it, but that's what's expected of us. The scientists, technologists, and their many fetishists are well prepared for such a response and well insulated from its force. As far as they're concerned, such a response is just the whining from the clergy that they've been hearing since the mid–nineteenth century. It's just religious fools in the way of scientific thought and progress. So, holding ethical fire for the moment, let us simply insist that a program such as *Beyond Human* is not a neutral, educational documentary on the subject of science in which the kind people at PBS help scientists to make nice to the rest of us. It is a narrative, a work of the social as well as the technological imagination, and it puts forward an argument—an argument that it is critical for us to understand before we respond. Abstracted from the flow of its documentary revelations, the argument in *Beyond Human* is what is called a "slippery slope" argument. Here is the implicit question, even though it is never directly posed: Is crossing the human/machine boundary a good or a bad thing?

The answer the PBS writers provide to their own implicit question is, "Well, is it wrong to use machines to help people in medical need? If a machine can help a blind person to see, is that a bad thing? And is it bad if the machine happens to be inside the person? Or inside the brain?"

The obliging viewer responds, "I see where you're coming from. All right. That's good enough for me."

Then the next step: "If it's not bad to implant devices to help the ill or disabled, there are other reasons, perhaps, for allowing the same thing. Would you agree?"

Obliging viewer: "Sure."

"And would you agree that it is important that our young fighting soldiers have every advantage to defeat the enemy and defend us and our precious liberties? After all, if nothing sacrosanct has been compromised in placing computer chips inside the disabled, why is it wrong to put them in soldiers? If we don't and a soldier is wounded, we might then have to put the device on after the fact, as a therapeutic, as we've already argued. But why wait until it's too late and the damage is done?"

"Wow. That's a really good point. Okay, implants and lasers and gadgets of every kind inside and outside our fighting men and women. I don't need disabled war vets on my conscience."

"And just what is it that our soldiers fight for? Our freedom? Our free enterprise system? Would you deny our culture the right to prosperity? If the economy is now dependent on technology and information, shouldn't we let it flow where it must, even if that means we're a little more machine-like, and the machines look a little more like Darwinian competition? You may be nervous about the ethical implications, but that's just one perspective. Americans love their technologies. Cars, TVs, games, stereos—they're all part of the fun and profit of being in this time in this place. You have no choice but to allow it. Why not relax and enjoy?"

"Gosh. You're probably right. I am a little uptight. If we're just going to shackle the economy with these unreasonable and antique ethical demands, what's the point of having our soldiers out there at all? Once again, they're off fighting for us, and we're back here undermining them. I'm really sorry. I completely concede."

And on we go by patient degrees until the obliging and maybe a little naive viewer arrives at a position he never would have assented to if it had been trotted out in the beginning.

"We made the machines. They are products of our minds. They are human in the sense that they're dependent on humans for the very possibility of their existence. Don't waste any tears over our demise if we're inferior to our own creations. The machines are simply the next evolutionary step for our own species. If they are us, in what sense are we extinct?"

"That's so incredibly profound. That is really deep. I think I love this vision, man."

"Wonderful. Here's a little present. It's a Nintendo NBA game. We've programmed a simulacrum of you into the game. In this game you can jump a full six inches higher than Michael Jordan can. In fact, you'll be replacing him in the starting lineup of the 1998 Chicago Bulls."

"Awesome!"

"We'll go one better than that. We're going to program a feed loop of you sinking the winning shot of game seven of the NBA Championship and load it into the mainframe aboard this spacecraft, which is taking all of the androids off to distant parts of the universe where their version of humanity will live on forever. You'll be sinking that shot into eternity."

"Can't ask for more than that!"

Wyndham Lewis long ago provided a pertinent perspective on the consequences of the popular relationship to techno-science:

> It is plainly the popularization of science that is responsible for the fever and instability apparent on all sides. To withhold knowledge from people, or to place unassimilable knowledge in their hands, are both equally effective, if you wish to render them helpless. (quoted in McLuhan, 92)

Technical rationality's desire to dominate nature is achieved only when nature is no more, not even the human nature that we're so "impatient" with. Ultimately, nature is fully controlled only when the last thing left on the field is the very apparatus of its control. An apparatus for mastery of something that no longer even exists.

I wish I could tell you that you don't have to take this story, or its undergraduate "slippery slope" logic, seriously. I wish I could tell you that it's just our good, mostly liberal friends at PBS educating us. I wish I could tell you that the well-funded scientists at Carnegie Mellon are off on some delusional trip with no real consequences. But the truth is that they're behaving as if they were in an arms race with themselves, and the insane point is to accelerate and push technical reasoning in a long, slow social suicide. But I can also tell you this, and perhaps it will lift your chin a bit. There is nothing inevitable about technology as social destiny. That fate is not internal to technology itself. That fate is elsewhere. Technology will not drag us to its Faustian destination if its *stories* are not good. Thus the real battle is at the level of the imagination. If other stories about the role of technology are stronger and more persuasive, a future "beyond human" won't happen. Unfortunately, the technophiles, those who think of technology as destiny, are not only good scientists; they're pretty sophisticated storytellers as well.

Take as a case in point Steven Spielberg's recent *AI*. You know that someone is serious about the imagination as a battlefront when he or she brings in Spielberg to crank the ideological juices. Like any other kind of politics, techno-science needs the appearance of legitimacy, needs the appearance of social consent as it spends billions of our tax dollars on the next generation of silicon chips, smart bombs, and androids. Spielberg's purpose (beyond making money and "entertaining") is very simple: he wants us to embrace techno-science both intellectually and emotionally. He will convince us to endorse techno-science by manipulating our emotions so that we feel we could "love" a machine. (Not such a far-fetched thing, really. How many of us have said that we loved "that old '51 Rambler"? Well, maybe not a Rambler.)

Spielberg's cinematographic logic works along these lines. *AI* is about artificial intelligence in a robot-boy, David, who has been programmed with real human emotions. In a crucial scene midway through the movie, robot-boy David is abandoned and then captured with other escaped and unlicensed robots out wandering the countryside. He is then taken to a "Flesh Fair." The Flesh Fair is part circus, part Roman coliseum, and part death camp. Before a crowd of howling, beer-guzzling, tattooed working-class people taken up in a frenzy of destruction amid heavy-metal guitar riffs (courtesy of Ministry), the robots are paraded forward, one by one, to be publicly destroyed in sadistic ways. Even little David, the first robot capable of human feeling, is to be destroyed.

Spielberg's contempt for the humans in this scene is not subtle. The humans are all booze, violence, raucous music, and bestial behavior. They are even by human measures plainly inferior to the robots who seem in contrast all Dickensian sensitivity. (In an interview in the DVD version of *AI*, Spielberg says that this scene is about "class conflict": the robots have been taking the jobs of the humans. It's revealing to know that this is how Spielberg sees the working class. If we can have 'bots like David, we're well rid of the brutes.) Clearly, if these Neanderthals can be convinced that a robot can be human, then anyone can be convinced. But in even more provocative ways, Spielberg is of course arguing to his own movie-going audience that we can and should care for machines.

The Flesh Fair has a vicious Irish emcee who persuades the crowd that David the robot-boy should be doused in acid and destroyed, because the 'bots have overpopulated the human world and are threatening to take the place of real children. They are eclipsing humans and should be annihilated. Spielberg counters this argument, implicitly, by depicting the Flesh Fair as like the slaughter of early Christians in the coliseum, as like the lynching of black men (the first robot to be destroyed is in blackface and minstrel garb; he is shot from a cannon, set on fire as he passes through a burning ring, and decimated by a spinning propeller), and, finally, as like the Jewish holocaust. As the robots line up in their cage before going to their fate, David asks, "Why is this happening?" The answer, "History repeats itself. It is the rite of blood and electricity." In other words, it's *Kristallnacht* for 'bots. Nazi rites of blood and soil are here transformed. Now, does Spielberg *really* believe that the destruction of machinery is like the murder of Christians, blacks, or Jews? Probably not. I sure hope not. But that is nonetheless the unmistakable narrative contour for this film. All is fair in ideological warfare. If the point is to say that we should care for machines, Spielberg has found a clever if demagogic way of doing it.

Of course, at just the moment that David is to be dissolved by a bucket of acid poured over his head, the nasty crowd turns suddenly rational and vaguely middle class. In response to David's cries for help, a woman stands and says, "Robots don't plead for their lives. It's a boy. Let him go." Empathy is achieved. The emcee's case is demolished, and he is stoned by a virtuous farmer-looking guy in overalls. (Stoned with beanbags? Why did everyone in this audience have a colored beanbag? Did they frequently stone the emcee? And why with colorful beanbags? For an instant, the film seems to lose its mind.) For the moment, Spielberg has succeeded in convincing his audience (both in and outside of the film) that machines are deserving of our care, and that those who treat them as less than deserving are the "moral equivalent" (as field marshal Reagan used to put it) of cruel Roman royalty, the KKK, and the Nazis. Technophobes and Luddites are reduced to a Brown Shirt goon squad. Resistance to technology is all beer, heavy metal, and animal violence.

Not a very subtle argument, but in Spielberg's hands, pretty effective.

The dangers of a cynical and manipulative film such as *AI* are obvious. I'd say that an innocuous-seeming program such as *Beyond Human* is also dangerous, never mind its "education channel" appeal to objectivity. But it is dangerous not because of some explicit threat within it (we're creating Frankensteins, etc.). *Beyond Human* is dangerous because of what it *doesn't* do. It doesn't do the kind of thinking that could persuade and assure its audience that techno-science can be trusted to be safe. The program does not oblige the techno-scientists it interviews to apply their thinking to themselves. Their machines may be capable of recursive functions, but the scientists themselves aren't. In philosophy, recursive thinking is known as "second-order thinking," and takes the form, first, of a truth-claim followed by the question, "How do we know what we think we know?" Second-order thinking is a man wearing a mask and pointing to the mask. It is philosophical self-revelation. A techno-science that could be trusted would not only present its creations; it would present a full ethical and social context within which to evaluate the desirability of those creations. It would be self-revealing rather than strategic.

Beyond Human and *AI* are both cunning in the way they make their arguments. They are not even willing to confess that in fact they are making arguments. They purport to be merely "documenting" or "entertaining." But the claim that we're somehow "impatient" with our bodies, which are "frozen in time" (whatever the hell that means), is an *argument*. It is probably strategically wise not to admit that it's an argument, because as an argument it is trivial. It is a mockery of thought. It is—one of my favorite words for things that are truly and surpassingly stupid—*jejune*. So, it's up to us, the people who will have to live with the consequences of their fertile inventiveness and their jejune thinking, to do the sort of careful consideration that is called for. The question there, of course, as I've said repeatedly, is whether or not we're in the least prepared to read and think and reimagine in our turn.

Given our chance, perhaps we ought to ask what happens to morality in this brave new world of machinelike humans for whom pain is absent or qualified (assuming that morality is premised upon an aversion to bodily pain, as is suggested by the fact that cutting off your neighbor's nose would result in a finding of "pain and suffering" for which you would be held legally and morally liable). What happens to concepts like cruelty? Spielberg would argue that we should extend our moral concepts to machines and make them the object of our caring. But it could just as easily, and more probably, work in the other direction. It could tend to erode human morality. In a culture organized around "systems" that are powerful precisely because they are independent of human individuals, what difference does the individual or his pain make so long as the *system* is preserved?

Given this complication, how does techno-science answer the question, "Why not be cruel?" Is chopping up robots in a propeller cruel? Spielberg seems to want to answer, "Yes, it is cruel, because they're like us." But this is, for real-world purposes, a laughable response. No one would take Spielberg's answer seriously outside of his cinematic artifice. The more reasonable response is that, no, it really doesn't matter what you do to them. They're not human. They're electronic junk. And the more it seems to us that our world is all composed of electronic junk, and that we're an extension of that electronic junk, the more it will seem that it's quite okay to blow it up, this world beyond humans, and any straggler humans with it. When an F-16 focuses its laser-guided ordnance on an Iraqi tank, what is the human component in this far-too-common scenario? Is the human component accessible to the pilot? To anyone save the poor guy's wife back in Baghdad?

For this brave new world, questions of cruelty don't need to be considered, because we're all just going into the technical future in some sort of inscrutably bland and contextless sense. Beyond the obvious but nonetheless absent moral questions, the program *Beyond Human*, like most popular presentations of the work of techno-science, utterly fails to ask who benefits and who loses from the work on cyborgs and androids. Gentlemen and ladies of technical science, in whose interest do you work? The impression is very directly given that science works for "us." As "we've" seen (you and I, reader), programs like *Beyond Human* strongly imply a collective but indistinct "we." But clearly not everyone benefits (or benefits equally) from the work of techno-science. So who are the winners and losers? What is the digital divide in these matters? If we knew these winners and losers, would they tend to reflect the old social evils of gendered occupations (the vast majority of scientists and technologists are still men), racism (blacks and Latinos are mostly left out of the new Information Economy), and imperialism (for many people in the Third World, their introduction to our techno-scientific achievements will be first experienced as one falls on their heads)?

Finally, who in our culture speaks against (or even about) the rationalized body of the beyond-human? In the past, poets worked in the creation of a very different understanding of the human body. They would speak metaphorically and metamorphically. An octopus has no bones or cartilage. Its body is fluid. It can flow its body into a bottle discarded on the ocean floor. It can change its skin color and texture to conform to whatever is around it. It imagines itself as rock, kelp, or rusted boot. In the mythology at the origin of Western culture, the human body is metamorphic in this way. In the legends of Ovid the body flows organically among other animate and inanimate objects such as deer, flowers, stars, and laurel trees. The human body is one with a larger universe. Humanity and the universe were imagined as interpenetrating. The character Proteus in Homer's *Odyssey* could change his body at will. Proteus was a "shape-shifter." Now human, now a lion.

But at present only Cultural Studies speaks in an engaged way about the body and is in any sort of position to challenge the assumptions of technical disembodiment. Unhappily, even its rhetoric is rationalized in the language of "discursive formations" and "social apparatuses." The theorist's proposition of the "body-as-text" quickly loses any potential critical edge to the imperatives of consumption. Cultural Studies' interest in the body has been all too easily made part of the chic, the hip, and the fashionable. Cultural Studies has not created artists and intellectuals of the body; it has created *flâneurs*, bohemians, what Walter Benjamin (in his *Arcades Project*) calls the first step in the fetishizing of the object as a consumable commodity, available in the shopping arcade or mall.[14] No sooner does the idea of body-as-text lead to the examination of tattoos than we're off to the parlor to purchase our own. Or the idea of body-building as discourse leads to a membership at Gold's Gym and not to a confrontation with the assumptions of the body as portrayed in *Beyond Human*.[15] The body-as-text is also a disembodied body, a rationalized body. Cultural

---

[14] See Benjamin's *The Arcades Project*, Harvard University Press, Cambridge, MA, 1999.

[15] I was at a conference on the postmodern text at Kent State a few years back at which a young and very buff female "scholar of the body" actually prefaced her essay by going through her body-building poses, shaved, tanned, and oiled. There were many there who could not avoid the conclusion that scholarship had at last arrived.

Studies cannot offer a counter-discourse but only a counter-rationalism to techno-rationalism. In other words, rationalism cannot lose in this battle. Cultural Studies' concession to rationalism in its choice of weapons is a tremendous victory in itself for rationalism. Cultural Studies is complicit with technical rationality at the level of its language, of its being. It is profoundly *not* the language of Wallace Stevens's "Domination of Black":

> At night, by the fire,
> The colors of the bushes,
> And of the fallen leaves,
> Repeating themselves,
> Turned in the room,
> Like the leaves themselves
> Turning in the wind.

I would not argue that the "shape-shifting" body of poetry is in some way a more "natural" consideration of the body. I would only say that it is a truer antagonist of the rationalized body. But, at present, frankly, poetry is not relevant. It's off with the quilting guilds in a very obscure corner of the culture dedicated to self-improvement and quality-of-life issues. Poetry has been reduced to a sort of Feng Shui for the mind.

Stevens once commented, quoting Nicolas Boileau-Despréaux, that "Descartes cut poetry's throat." Two and a half centuries later, Theodor Adorno felt compelled to say, "After Auschwitz, poetry is impossible." The relationship between these two comments describes a trajectory and acceleration of instrumental rationality, the general rationalizing and disembodying of the human world. For the authors of Auschwitz, the Jews were first and foremost what they *thought*. (Most conspicuously, they failed to think that Aryans were a superior race.) That the Jews were attached to bodies was incidental for the Nazis. The Jews simply had the wrong idea. The bodies of the Jews were mere "puppets" or "baggage." In the nightmare of post-humanity, our bodies are fashion accessories. Or, as novelist William Gibson puts it in *Neuromancer*, our bodies are "meat puppets," merely those things through which we "jack in" to the Virtual World, the infinite and infinitely abstract Web. Clearly the rationalizing process inaugurated by Descartes has not played itself out. And yet all of this has come to be, for our latest generation of scholars, scientists, and techno-aficionados, imponderably cool. Hip. But this is surely what media critic Mark Crispin Miller calls "the hipness unto death."

In Adam Smith's famous rendering of capitalism, Smith claims that private vice (greed) leads to public benefits (prosperity). In the world of techno-science, private virtue (scientific invention) leads to public disaster (a technological society above and beyond all question and in the service of a global economic and military system). As Helen Caldicott describes in relation to the work of nuclear scientists, "Thousands of physicists, chemists, and engineers—the cream of the crop, recruited from U.S. colleges over a period of sixty years—brilliant, rational, careful, strictly scientific, engaged in exploring the very elements of creation, and all committed to the design, construction, and testing of nuclear weapons." (14) But, as Paul Virilio observes wisely, this brilliance may in the end be tragic, because "knowing how to do it doesn't mean we know what we are doing." (63)

A last comment on androids before moving on. They, the androids, may already be with us. Here in Normal, Illinois, I listen to NOAA weather radio. For the last few years, the bored-stupid humans who used to have to recite the same damned weather 24/7 have been relieved by a computer voice. The thing is, when the voice says, for instance, that Tuesday will be "cloudy," it sounds so mournful. I sometimes imagine that the speaker is depressed. He—it's a male voice—says it like this, "clow-dee," in a deep, falling timbre. I think the monotony of the job is getting to him. I think he's had it with the weather, one day after another. Cloud after sun before rain and always more wind. It's endless and pointless, and I think the little computer man is figuring it out—and a lot quicker than the humans that preceded him.

This year he has been joined by a female computer voice. I guess we think that all occupations should be equally appropriate and equally open to both male and female computer voices. What a wonderful country! But me, I'm thinking, "That computer guy is depressing, but this computer chick is a hotty! She comes to me in images of plastic bliss." Plastic fantastic lover, indeed. Then I think, "Okay, there they are all alone back at the NOAA weather station in Wichita, Kansas, or wherever the hot hell it is, and what do they do? Maybe they're getting it on. I don't know. Could be. Maybe this is how the robots are going to reproduce themselves and replace us. It's all going to start with the weather computer people. Perhaps the future won't be so bad after all. Maybe the computers will let us watch. It's the least they could do."

5.

I will close these considerations of the political and technological imaginations with an example of what stands opposed to them, however frailly. It is an ever-wayward, iconoclastic, reluctant (if not resistant), and intellectually nomadic North American mind that situates itself between technology and its opposition. True heir to Laurence Sterne's *Tristram Shandy*, it seeks to digress its way to freedom.

As I have attempted to make clear, the critical point is neither to be pro nor to be contra technology. The issue is how technology is taken up in the social imagination. Sick social, sick technology. Mike Heppner's 2002 novel *The Egg Code* illustrates not only an alternative to the sterility of the technophile/phobe dualism; it also reveals just how difficult it is to create a position that succeeds in truly detaching itself from the situation it would like to critique. It is about the difficulty of working in a context in which the efforts of individuals, no matter how adversarial their intentions, are made useful to the interests of a larger and dominating reality or system.

The main plot of *The Egg Code* is a rather science-fictive device having to do with the Gloria Corporation. Gloria is a router. Routers, we are told in the first chapter, are "specialized computers designed to control the flow of traffic." (8) Gloria's insidious coup is that it has managed to manipulate all the other routers in the country to run through it. So it is now the *über*-router. Gloria's high-tech empire is a digital enterprise gone viral. She is the iron queen of the Nano Age. Although there are squads of human goons scurrying to protect Gloria's interests, there is no human in charge. This is a version of the beyond-human that seems almost familiar. A nation of Web junkies, we have "servers" on which we are pathologically dependent. There are no robots here, but there is a technologically entrenched system for which all humans feel an obligation to work, regardless of its effect on what we used to call human society.

Up against this cartoonish high-tech villain is an array of characters, most of whom are operating in ignorance of the activities of the others (putting them at a distinct disadvantage to Gloria), and all of whom in one way or another are trying to defeat Gloria. This cast begins with the publisher, Bart Hasse, descendent of the original Gutenberg, who is determined to destroy the Internet and keep information "something physical, something you could touch." (59) Interestingly, the anti-digital Hasse is certainly the most distasteful and unscrupulous human in the book. For instance, Hasse is quite comfortable pimping his daughter as a part of his strategy to preserve the book. There is also Martin Field, a computer engineer of great genius who is seduced by Bart Hasse's daughter (at her father's instruction) in order to blackmail him into doing work that has the intended effect of undermining Gloria, although it is also clear that that is not what he accomplishes. Martin's son, Olden, sets up a hacker's den from which he constructs a site called the Egg Code. His strategy is to sow false information so broadly on the Internet that the Net's credibility is ruined. What he discovers is that passing erroneous information is exactly the method that Gloria itself uses to bring other devices into its web. This failure leads him to retreat to the Luddite technique of simply trying to blow Gloria up.

What these characters and many more learn is that no matter

what they do, no matter how combative their intent, their efforts all end up affirming Gloria. These characters conspire against themselves. As one character puts it, "Do you believe that others like you may have inadvertently contributed to a harmful mindset in this country?" To which the answer is, "Yes, dear, I do. I think about it all the time. It fills me with a terror that I can't describe." (38)

This engaging and lively plot is both a serious attempt to confront current cultural issues and an *X-Files* conspiracy-theory spoof. But *The Egg Code* is not entirely serious about its plot. We know this in part because Heppner jokes with the reader about the old writing lesson, "If a pistol is revealed in the first act, it had better go off in the last act." One Scarlet Blessing, a charmingly deranged young woman, repeatedly pulls a gun from her backpack, but the gun is conspicuously never used. *The Egg Code* has a more material strategy for engaging the problems of cyber-culture. The material book itself is a test of the contrary forces of digital infomatics and the tradition of the book. The design and structure of the book is fragmented, a-chronological, and, in a word, hypertextual. The multiple plot lines and complex character relations could best be described by a graph showing the hyperlinks. Against the novel's hypertextuality Heppner asserts the pleasures of book textuality in the old-fashioned sense. Our pleasure in the novel comes from Heppner's astonishing formal inventiveness, his consistent metaphoric resourcefulness, his love of words and syntax, his superb ear for voice and dialogue, and his wonderful sense of humor. In the plot, Gloria wins. But for this novel as a whole, the Word wins out over all computers and empires because Heppner makes Literary Invention the real hero. In his postmodern way, Heppner revels in a vital stubbornness to maintain what is finally a centuries-old human ideal of creativity.

As I emphasized in my comments on Adorno's aesthetic, art can show us how freedom can be rediscovered and reclaimed in the context of unfreedom. It can *lead*. But ultimately an art that is only a commodity, only something for sale at Barnes & Noble (and, through no fault of his own, Heppner's book is not much more than that), is no alternative at all. The art of the sixties was potent because it was part of a much broader social effort to reinvent the social world. Art and the social imagination played a purposeful game of mutual provocation, constantly upping the ante, one challenging the other. So consequential was this game that it very nearly led to the fall of governments in France, Italy, and even, at certain moments, the United States. It is not too much to say that the call to the imagination from those moments, broadcast through underground culture as "samizdat," had a crucial role in the fall of the Soviet Union. That capitalism in the West succeeded in routing this inventive energy back to its imperatives is inevitably part of the story. The question for us in the present is how to make the work of an artist like Heppner something more than a sad reminder of just how desiccated our world is now. The question is how to socialize his energy.

Chapter 4

THE HIGHWAY OF DESPAIR
LEADS TO
A WORLD IN LOVE

Looking back at some dead world that looked so new.
Beck

1.

I think it is critical to the plausibility of my argument to show that, in essence, I am not the only one who has noticed something amiss with our national imagination, that there are others who have not only noticed but are working constructively to reclaim authority over the creation of the human world. These efforts are no doubt multiple and manifold if not universally visible.

One such sustained effort to create a sort of ongoing "separate reality" has been the New Age movement. Rooted in the counterculture's fascination with the occult and with Eastern religion, New Age (in conjunction with the self-help, human potential, and recovery movements) has claimed that contemporary American life is toxic, stifling, spiritually debasing, and contrary to the goal of whole, creative individuals in a healthy, spiritually attuned human and natural world. These tenets, which have found astonishingly broad consensus, especially among well-educated, affluent North Americans, are at heart a response to what Marx called "alienation." Capitalism alienates workers from their true capacity as humans. Whether or not it is an *adequate* response is another question. One way or the other, the literature of the New Age movement, especially as it engages issues of creativity, provides a revealing instance of the social forces I have been describing in full engagement.

I want to look at Julia Cameron's hugely successful book *The Artist's Way: A Spiritual Path to Higher Creativity* (1992). It has sold over two million copies over a ten-year period, spinning off no fewer than twelve subsequent books, journals, and workbooks. Cameron has almost single-handedly created a self-help creativity industry. At first glance, *The Artist's Way* appears merely opportunistic, drawing from a broad variety of alternatives in contemporary therapeutic culture. For example, Cameron appeals to the logic of Alcoholics Anonymous (*The Artist's Way* has twelve chapters, just as AA has twelve steps) and the literature of "recovery." She refers to her audience as "recovering creatives"—recovering, that is, from being "blocked."

This is a curious take on the idea of "writer's block," because it looks back to the antique idea that creativity comes from a "muse," a transcendental sprite that delivers the creative goodies. For Cameron, a block is therefore a spiritual problem. God ("as you understand that word," as the recovery movement likes to put it) is a creative principle, and S/He means to flow through us. But when food, sex, drugs, and work all function as toxic impediments to our creativity, we become blocked. In response, Cameron provides tasks, daily writings, and what she calls "artist dates" to return the toxic artist to a pure state as spiritual channel for God's creativity.

There is very little new in Cameron's thinking, save for the idea that everyone has an artist within that wants to create. (This is said in much the same way that Buddhists argue that every person contains *bodhicitta*, the wisdom of the Buddha, in potential.) We have seen Cameron's approach applied in a variety of contexts over the last three decades, even in "self-help" books like W. Timothy Gallwey's *The Inner Game of Tennis*, which helped to start the now enormous area of "sports psychology." Gallwey argued that we have two selves: a natural, learning self (self 2) and a censorial, critical, controlling self (self 1) that makes it difficult for self 2 to perform. Needless to say, Gallwey (along with Cameron and everyone else in New Age) thinks that as a nation we're dominated by control-freak self 1, and we need to "get in touch" with the pure principle of innate capacity represented by self 2. This is what Phil Jackson is talking to Shaq and Kobe about when he says, "Stay in the moment." Cameron reasons in a similar vein that our creative self is crippled by the negativity produced by our inner censor, who says meanly derogatory things like, "You think you're a writer!? You can't even spell!"

Also present in Cameron's New Age/self-help/recovery lexicon are inner child therapy, meditation, human potential, sexual abuse therapy, personal affirmation practice, self-parenting, spiritual chiropractic, and oneness with the universe. This potpourri of problems and strategies is so open to inclusion that it even encompasses a little old-fashioned Calvinism, as when Cameron claims that getting in touch with and unblocking the inner artist leads to worldly success: "When we do what we are meant to do, money comes to us, doors open for us, we feel useful, and the work we do seems like play to us." (108)

Although much of what Cameron describes could be material for an Al Franken/Stuart Smalley skit (imagine Smalley peering earnestly into his little mirror and saying, "I am a talented person. I have a right to be an artist. I am a good person and a good artist" [Cameron, 146]), it is also important to say that much of what Cameron describes is related to a very necessary critique of capitalist/corporate/consumer culture. While Cameron's book is an alternative *within* Western corporate culture and not a rejection of that culture, she unmistakably identifies work, money, and TV as primary culprits in blocked creativity. Cameron's call to her audience is to reclaim its human right to creativity, to an expansion of possibility, and to the playful libidinization of all life. In opposition to the "numbing" provided by the TV drug, Cameron proposes "rearrangement" of everything from the furniture to fundamental values. There *is* something radical about her thought, even if she cannot be described as in full flight from the dominant culture.

This is a point that Andrew Ross makes with great acuity in writing about the politics of New Age in *Strange Weather* (1991):

The small-scale imperative of New Age's cooperative commu-
nitarianism brings with it a host of potentially critical positions: against big, centralized bureaucracies; against big,
transnational business conglomerates; against large-scale, and
environmentally destructive, technologies; against the imperialist claims made on the basis of strong nationalism; and
against monolithic institutions in education, industry, religion
and the nuclear family. (69)

Also present in Cameron's construction of our world, unfortunately, is the great compromise with the reigning order of things that I
have referred to as the Middle Mind. Insofar as any of the projects I
have spoken of as typical of the Middle Mind are oppositions to the
status quo, they are an opposition in the image of the thing they would
contest. And so New Age's great failing is that its difference is a sameness, and from its inception. In the case of Julia Cameron and *The
Artist's Way*, this sameness is conspicuous.

As Terry Gross does on *Fresh Air*, Cameron flattens all distinctions. Everyone is an artist. Everyone is capable of making good art.
Everyone, as she says in her best Stuart Smalley voice, has a
"snowflake pattern" in his or her soul, and "each of us is a unique, creative individual." (85) Once our creativity is discovered, "there may
even be bursts of spontaneous singing, dancing, running."[1] (84) This,
once again, is the All is One of romanticism, the night in which all
cows are black, the death of discrimination. It is a feel-good aesthetic,
and a no-one-gets-hurt aesthetic. The distinction that Cameron fails to
make is the difference between the idea of art as we have discovered it
in Adorno and Shklovsky (critics for whom difference meant everything) and a very separate idea of what we might call, utopically, everyday creativity. Mundane creativity. Art as it is understood by Feng

---

[1] I'm reminded of Jules Feiffer's aery creatives, garbed in leotards, leaping across
the cartoon frames in creative majesty.

Shui. Rearranging the furniture, to use Cameron's example, may be a creative act, but it is not necessarily an artistic act. This discrimination eludes Cameron.

Cameron also fails to provide a context for her diagnoses. She is willing to suggest that work, money, TV, and drugs are problems, but she is not willing to take the next step and relate these problems to a larger social order. And for a good reason: while she may be willing to find our culture full of potential toxins and blocks, she is not willing to suggest that we need to create an alternative culture beyond the status quo. Rather, her suggestion is that we find ways of making ourselves *individually* well within it. This is Cameron's most alarming self-contradiction. She repeatedly affirms the world of Hollywood, the Emmys, big-city book reviews, and traditional commercial measures of success as the legitimate aspiration of the "inner artist." A case in point: "Ginny, a writer-producer, credits the morning pages with inspiration for her recent screenplays and clarity in planning her network specials." (9) Well, I'm glad to learn that *someone* associates inner clarity with network specials!

For Cameron, artists are people like Steven Spielberg, who "claims that his very best ideas come to him as he was [*sic*] driving the freeways." (23) (Probably the same freeway where Lycos creator Bob Davis got his ideas about speed and life.) In general Cameron encourages her devotees to seek wholeness in the very world that is the source of their toxicity: corporate culture. This strikes me as being in very bad faith, and it comes in spite of the fact that Cameron herself was once so frustrated with the studio system in Hollywood, which had repeatedly failed to produce her work, that she created her own independent production company. Of course, she then measured the success of her company by all the standard, mainstream devices—reviews, awards, and money. (Cameron is insistent that artists should not be afraid of money.) It seems to me, though, that Cameron has failed to learn something that the dominant culture was trying very hard to teach her: autonomy.

If the Artist's Way were the teaching of a Buddhist school, it would be Hinayanist as opposed to Mahayanist. In Hinayana, the

Buddha-in-the-making, an *arhat*, saves herself. In Mahayana, the Buddha-to-be, a *bodhisattva*, returns to the world of suffering and change out of compassion for others. Cameron seeks to help people (educated, affluent people with the time on their hands to indulge in New Age self-realization exercises) to make their separate peace with the world as it is. An easy thing for the affluent to do, I should think. By so doing, she ensures that there will never be a lack of toxic or otherwise damaged human beings. But after all, what good is a therapeutic movement without a disease? In the Artist's Way, the cure protects the disease.

Of course, there is no need for these subtleties to see Cameron's complicity with that which she would seem to be in combat. To judge that complicity, all you need to do is look at the cover: her book comes in the gold and red of pulp romance novels. The title is embossed as on cheap bodice-rippers, as if Cameron's readers might like to read it in Braille. And on the very last page, her dirty little secret: the Artist's Way is a registered trademark; it is an industry unto itself. Cameron has produced a dozen books and spin-off products for the suffering inner artist. Does anyone detect that old-timey aroma of snake oil?

No wonder Cameron thinks so well of money for artists.

2.

While there are some, like Julia Cameron, who are in general agreement with my account of the impoverished and damaged state of our social imagination (however different our diagnoses and prescriptions), there are others who have argued recently that just the opposite is the case. Richard Florida, in his book *The Rise of the Creative Class* (2002), argues that in fact we are in what he calls the Creative Age. He reasons that the so-called Information Economy is in reality a Creative Economy. We have shifted "to an economic and social system based on human creativity." (15) Creativity is "the defining feature of economic life," Florida says. (21) In Florida's view, capitalism has trumped Karl Marx. If Marx saw that one of the primary grievances against capitalism was the way in which it alienated humans from their true capacities, well, *mirabile dictu*, in the end capitalism agreed with him. Capitalism discovered circa 1990 that it could be more profitable if it allowed workers to be creative. According to Florida, the most far-reaching (if only dimly plausible) consequence of this movement is that the proletariat now owns the "means of production":

> To some degree, Karl Marx had it partly right when he foresaw that workers would someday control the means of production. This is now beginning to happen, although not as Marx thought it would, with the proletariat rising to take over factories. Rather, more workers than ever control the means of production because it is inside their heads; they *are* the means of production. (37)

In Florida's vision, the new Creative Age is made possible by the three Ts: technology, talent, and tolerance. (You can tell that Florida has made a lot of PowerPoint presentations to regional economic planners. I can practically see the big scarlet Ts come up on the screen, red and perfect and inevitable.) Technology means, basically, Silicon Valley, the high-tech industry. Talent is held by the creative geek (that mythical creature that constitutes the new mainstream: "neither outsider nor insider, neither bohemian nor bourgeois, the geek is simply a technologically creative person" [210]). The geeks make technology productive. The final T, tolerance, is the diversity of people and cultures that makes communities attractive to the creative geeks. Geeks want to live in diverse communities and will seek employment only in these "creative centers." These three qualities together, for Florida, have produced capitalism's most recent large-scale economic transformation.

The primary beneficiaries of the new economy have been the creative individuals involved. They constitute a supercreative core of scientists, artists, musicians, writers, and software developers, as well as a peripheral community of "creative professionals" who "work in a wide range of knowledge intensive industries such as high-tech sectors, financial services, the legal and healthcare professions and business management." (69) At times Florida's enthusiasm for our creativity becomes so broad that it seems everyone is a little creative—even copy-machine technicians, who "acquire their own arcane bodies of knowledge and develop their own unique ways of doing the job." (70)

According to Florida's figures, the creative class now constitutes 30 percent of employees. The remaining 70 percent comes from agriculture (1 percent), the working class (26 percent), and, conspicuously, a huge and ever-growing service class (43 percent). The growth of low-pay, low-creativity service-class jobs over the last two decades has also been driven by the creativity boom, because the creative class requires someone else to do its cooking, cleaning, and childcare while it puts in its sixty-hour weeks. The service class is like an "outsourced" servant working on contract. In fact, outsourcing is one of the most salient features of the Creative Economy across the board. Creative workers tend to have what Florida calls "horizontal" careers. That is, they move from employer to employer. They are more interested in the challenge of specific projects than in the benefits of a lifelong relationship with a single employer. The benefit to the employer is conspicuous: the company is not responsible to the employee for health insurance and other traditional benefits of employment. As Florida puts it, more grimly than I think he understands, "We acknowledge that there is no corporation or other large institution that will take care of us—that we are truly on our own." (115) This, clearly, is the new economy's version of Rugged Individualism. Those geeks are tough bastards after all.

From a national perspective it works like this: deregulation makes corporations less responsible to the government (which, you might recall, is supposed to be of, by, and for us), while outsourcing makes them less responsible to their employees. This is a huge win-win for corporations, the first achieved during the Reagan administration, the second during the Clinton years. Further, service-sector outsourcing makes the creative class less responsible, in its turn, for its newly conceived servants. The servant class, finally, is content with dull, low-paying jobs, perhaps because they are at least clean and safe and better than the dangerous and tedious factory jobs that workers in Mexico and Indonesia endure—workers for whom, it would appear, nobody in the wide world needs to feel responsible. This passing down of social and ethical responsibility—of any sense that as a community we are each other's keepers—ends as it always has since Marx's first descriptions of workers so poor that their only property was their own bodies: in the dirt of poverty and hopelessness. The fact that contemporary capital has kindly arranged through globalism that we shouldn't have to see this poverty doesn't alter our dependence on their work, nor does it remove our ultimate complicity and culpability.

Florida's general narrative of how the Creative Economy came about is related to older narratives about how the hippies became yuppies and how, in David Brooks's formulation in *Bobos in Paradise*, bohemians and the bourgeois melded into "bobos." Florida's contribution to the story is to show that this movement is finally about fundamental economic trends and not merely about lifestyle decisions. It is impossible to deny that there have been fundamental changes in the economy in the United States over the last twenty years, or that there have been fundamental changes in the nature of work. There is even a great deal of plausibility in Florida's construction of how all this came about. It was a consequence of the sixties, just as Brooks and others have surmised. As Florida writes,

> The great cultural legacy of the sixties, as it turned out, was not Woodstock after all, but something that had evolved at the other end of the continent. It was Silicon Valley. . . . [The creative economy] engages the world of work and the world of life and weaves them together, profoundly changing both. (202)

In short, as Antonio Negri and Michael Hardt write in *Empire* (2001), the sixties created a demand for creativity in work. As they see it,

> "Dropping out" was really a poor conception of what was going on in the Haight-Ashbury and across the United States in the 1960s. The two essential operations were the refusal of the disciplinary regime and the experimentation with new forms of productivity. (274)

This refusal led to a transformation of labor power defined by "mobility, flexibility, knowledge, communication, [and] cooperation" (275) in the transformation of capitalist production in the subsequent decades. Clearly, from very different vantages, Hardt/Negri and Florida are looking at the same creature.

Florida is also right to connect this development in the economy to the changes we've seen in the affluent communities near centers of high-tech productivity—places like San Francisco, Austin, Seattle, and Portland. Florida's argument, of special pertinence to regional planners, is that if you want to be part of the prosperous future, you need to provide a stimulating and creative environment full of many ethnicities, gays and lesbians, international and gourmet foods, natural resources for hiking and recreation, and arts. A city with these attractions is the kind of place creative people want to live in, and no job is sufficiently remunerative to cause the core of the creative class to sacrifice these amenities and live in some southern or high-plains backwater mono-culture. The creative class demands stimulating "amenities," to use Florida's term: "What they are looking for in communities are abundant high-quality amenities and experiences, an openness to diversity of all kinds, and above all else the opportunity to validate their identities as creative persons." (218)

The only downside that Florida sees in the Creative Economy is the tendency to make some regions very wealthy (the West Coast, the East Coast, and university towns in between), while others are left out. He also worries about a race division in the new economy. Blacks and

Latinos will tend to be on the wrong side of the digital divide and take their unequal place in low-paying, low-creativity service jobs.[2] But there are other significant problems, both political and ethical, with Florida's argument—problems that he is much less willing or able to recognize or engage.

While *The Rise of the Creative Class* is a smart and well-researched book, a book resting on the bedrock of scholarly "best practices" of surveys, interviews, and focus groups, it fails conspicuously at the level of the imagination. There are obvious questions that Florida refuses to ask. This is the sort of book that, if it had a door, the reader would be banging on it, trying to get the author's attention (while the author is engrossed in downloading some really revealing graphs) so that she can say, "Hey, what about . . . ?" *The Rise of the Creative Class* is a revealing example of the imaginative limits of the very creativity it seeks to celebrate. There are limits beyond which Florida dares not think. For example, not once does he pause to consider the relations of the Creative Economy to realities in the global economy. Is the privilege of North American creative work in any way dependent on the exportation of factory jobs to the Third World? Pushed on this point, Florida would probably claim that the relation of our domestic creative economy to the international market is not a bad thing.

In some quarters, the idea of the United States, Japan, and Germany as centers of creative work in a larger world system is a strong assumption. The creative economy is part of what Richard Rosecrance describes as the "virtual state." In his 1999 book *The Rise of the Virtual State*, Rosecrance claims that the new international economic and political order has generated "head" nations and "body" nations. The head nations do the creative and service work described by Florida. The body nations do

---

[2] If, by Florida's own account, the service class has grown just as fast as the creative class and is in fact larger, and if, by Florida's own account, it operates as an outsourced set of servants doing the "chores" of bobo creatives, why (I have to wonder) doesn't he call the book *The Rise of the Servant Class?* Or, better yet, *The Rise of the Sinking Class?* Now there's something to celebrate and sell to regional planners!

manufacturing based upon the designs and strategies created in head nations. But this does not imply, for Rosecrance, an imperial relationship of rich northern over poor southern countries. In the virtual state, the military withers away because it is not needed in an economy that is about "flows of production and purchasing power rather than stocks of goods." (5) This body/head metaphor replaces the privileged/exploited model of international relations. Sure, if the world is just one big body, some of us will have to function as arms and legs, while others will have the clean (and clearly more prestigious and profitable) work of the head. Some, I take it, will have to be the intestines of this new international body. We'll be able to dump toxic shit in intestine nations just as we presently export our broken or outdated computers and electronic junk to Indonesia and other parts south, where the poor can pick through the pieces while heavy metals and other toxins percolate down into the groundwater.

Pure apologists for the emerging New World Order, both Florida and Rosecrance hold out the hope that in time we can all be creative workers. In time, we can all live in head countries. For Rosecrance, the system requires trust between foreign and domestic corporations and foreign and domestic governments. The question for us is, simply, Is there any reason provided by the history of capitalism to make us think that "trust" in an eventual world creativity is a well-placed trust?

Further, not once does Florida pause to wonder what the relation of this high-tech creativity is to militarism and the projection of military power into the larger world. One wants to ask, What is the responsibility of these software creatives for the earth-at-risk, hair-trigger nuclear reality that Helen Caldicott describes in her book *The New Nuclear Danger?* Florida's world is limited to "regions" of the United States. These are the blinders on his imagination. When it comes to fundamental economic realities, Florida must beg the question and assume that the reigning global economic system is a desirable one.

But even with the things that he does allow himself to talk about, there are enormous gaps in his thought. For example, what, Professor Florida, do you mean by art? Florida describes a function for the arts in the Creative Economy, but how does that function relate to the real social purpose of the arts? In short, what is the Creative Economy's aesthetic? The answers that Florida provides to this question are implicit and mostly disturbing. By and large, the function of the arts in the Creative Economy is to create a stimulating environment to attract high-tech industry and affluent creative workers to specific creative centers. The arts contribute to an "underlying eco-system" for creativity. "By supporting lifestyle and cultural institutions like a cutting-edge music scene or vibrant artistic community [for the trite of mind, good art is always *vibrant,* as if what we really had in mind was a Las Vegas floor show with lots of lights and *vibrations*] . . . it helps to attract and stimulate those who create in business and technology." (55)

It is easy to imagine this economic justification for the arts, and easy to imagine a regional planner being persuaded by it, but does the argument have anything to do with the concept of art, especially in its relation to the social? The bottom line—and Florida's book is ultimately all bottom line—is that the arts are a necessary part of the Creative Economy because creative workers (read: software engineers) demand the stimulation and experience of music and theater just as much as they demand an afternoon latte. Art is a lifestyle amenity that is tolerated and encouraged by business because it is, in the final reckoning, profitable. Creative centers like San Francisco are "entertainment machines." The progress and productivity that the Creative Economy gives us is indistinguishable from profit, finally. The Creative Economy is a money dialectic. Any art that is "stimulating" enough to make the creative workers happy and profitable is good art by this logic. So central is stimulation to art's social good, from Florida's perspective, that you'd think he had art confused with coffee.

This economic justification for the arts is like the yoga DVDs that are being sold for stress reduction. You put in the DVD, stretch, relax, and get ready for another day at the corporate cubicle in Dilbert-land. The Creative Economy likes yoga and likes art because they make smart workers available and productive. Art's truth and yoga's truth are irrelevant. Who cares what they really are? Let the professors worry about that. This is how we economic planners are going to use them. It's business pragmatism. And so I might as well just relax, I suppose. Breathe deep. See the CEO of the software startup company move into Mountain Position. He breathes in. He breathes out. He is entirely within the creative moment. Dollars puddle at his feet. It's Calvinism with a guru.

To those who would argue that taking art into a purely economic rationality kills its political potential, Florida replies aggressively:

> This absurd notion does a disservice to both politics and art. True political movements, from the civil rights movement to the grassroots organizing of the right wing, are serious entities, laboriously put together and directed to specific political ends. These movements sometimes adopt art forms but are not generated by them. Meanwhile, most good graffiti artists and rappers are like good artists of any kind. They mainly want to hone their skills and do their art. They spend a lot of time practicing, as you may know if you live near any. If they can make a little money in the process, that's wonderful. (201)

What curious creatures these artists must be! They're like little organ-grinder monkeys that love the music and love to dance their little dances all day long, and if you put a penny in their cup, why, they tip their little hats to you!

If your vision of art is that it exists in order to amuse techno-geeks as an inducement to work profitably, then this is a perfectly reasonable aesthetic. But even this debased notion of art runs into little problems with reality, as recent events in liberal Santa Cruz, California, have revealed. Santa Cruz has Florida's three Ts in abundance. It's a university town with a rich culture and a colorful past, and it neighbors Silicon Valley. And yet, as the Associated Press reported on September 23, 2002, all is not well with the artists and musicians that have, according to Florida, provided the cultural cool which allows Santa Cruz to be part of the Creative Economy.

> There are bad vibes downtown these days in this liberal beach town.

City leaders, frustrated by aggressive beggars and obnoxious sidewalk behavior, want to ban Hacky Sack games, sign-holding panhandlers after sundown and street music.

As a result, topless women, Uncle Sam on stilts, and Grateful Dead fans have been marching past surf shops, book stores and cafes chanting: "We're here, we're poor, we're not going shopping."

File this story under "Trouble in Creative Economy Paradise." The events in Santa Cruz are evidence of contradictions in the system. The Creative Economy, too, is dependent on the existence of a class of very poor and excluded people. As always, this is not a contradiction that can be repressed indefinitely.

Florida's theory of the Creative Economy presents a magnificent example of capitalism's ability to create an opposition in its own image. Do workers demand creativity? Okay, then, we'll give them creativity, but on our terms. The conscienceless creativity of techno-science is a fraud. What the creative class really represents is vocationalism. Art and creativity are made to pay their own way. And what's wrong with that? What's wrong with making a buck? What's wrong with carrying your own weight? The wrong, as I've said repeatedly, is that the vocationalizing of creativity has the tendency to impoverish the imagination and thereby impoverish the imagination's most basic social functions: to critique and to imagine alternatives to the social status quo. The imagination is really at work only when it is biting the hand that feeds it.

I recently visited Frank Lloyd Wright's first home and studio in Oak Park, Illinois, with my daughter, Megan. Afterward, in response to a comment I made about the site, she asked me what I meant by the *imagination*. I said, "You were just in it." Frank Lloyd Wright refused the human world of Victorian architecture (nice as that now seems to us in our vinyl-clad suburban horrors) and proposed an alternative way of using architecture to think about what kind of world humans ought to live in. As Wright himself said, "Every house is a missionary. I don't build a house without seeing the end of the present social order." And

all this Wright did in conservative Oak Park, looking at the prairie out
his studio windows.

Art and the imagination do not require stimulating urban centers,
yuppie amenities, and entertainments. People having to make a devil's
bargain might need these things as beggarly compensation for living
under an otherwise unacceptable economic reign. Capitalism proposes, "You give us your creative capacity and we'll give you these
amenities and the money to buy them with." The Creative Economy
does not require us to be artists. It requires us to be stupid-smart. It
used to be that we required only our soldiers to be stupid/smart —
dumb enough to go to Saigon, say, but smart enough to win once they
got there. Now workers need to be smart enough to want to be creative
and smart enough to be capable of creativity, but they also have to be
stupid enough to think that the present economic disposition really allows for this creativity. In the final analysis, our creativity will be *accounted*. As Florida writes, in a passage that sounds like doom to me:

> Some of these companies, like Motorola, take a page from
> Japanese-style quality management and actively manage and
> account for creativity. A system called the Capability Maturity
> Model (CMM), developed at the Software Engineering Insti-
> tute at Carnegie Mellon, lays out extensive standards and
> guidelines for managing software developers, a special class of
> creative workers. (129)

What are our high-tech creatives creating? Their own manacles.[3]

---

[3] On the subject of manacles, Florida repeatedly invokes Bloomington, Illinois
(better known as Bloomington-Normal), as one of the rising creative centers of the
new Creative Economy. I've lived here twenty-three years and I have no idea what
he's talking about. It's true that we have a large white-collar employment base, thanks
to State Farm Insurance and two universities, but there is little to no high-tech industry. Many of my students, over the years, have graduated from Illinois State and sought
their first employment at State Farm. It is not a thrilling prospect for them. It is not a
step into the great world of creative work. Employment at State Farm is universally referred to, in these parts, as "the golden handcuffs."

3.

So, where do we start to change the depressing destination that the technological imagination in particular and all of our accumulated failures of imagination in general, including Richard Florida's dispiriting ideas about creativity, have in mind for us? We ought to begin by recognizing that techno-science (including the creations of the new geek creative class), in consort with the narratives provided by global capital and a global military class, provides no historical or conceptual context for understanding where we've been, where we are, and where we're headed. In short, they collectively refuse thought. We need to provide that larger context. We need to think.

It should come as no surprise by this point that my own idea of context is substantially provided by a narrative beginning with the Enlightenment story of emancipation and universal justice. Much as they have been disparaged, Hegel and Marx were first and foremost philosophers of the late Enlightenment, deepening and providing rich material particularity—"content," as Hegel liked to put it—for the social situation in which emancipation can and should work. Their story is one of freedom, ethical community, and the end of exploitation. Hegel, in particular, advocated the end of the exploitation of humans in his critique of the "master/slave" relationship. He argued that in the end the only ethical human condition is the mutual, shared, respectful, civic recognition of human interdependence. This vision, as I hope to argue in this chapter, is an ultimately *spiritual* vision. To talk about these things is to talk about religion. For Hegel, spirit was not something existing in a superior or transcendental realm. It was exactly the condition of our social lives in a given moment; it was exactly what we think and do. If our culture is corrupt, cynical, and cruel, that is exactly what our spirit is. In Hegel's thought, corruption, cynicism, and cruelty cannot endure for the simple reason that they are inadequate to our true end: freedom. Freedom, in this tradition, is the ultimate openness to human possibility. The gap between what we want and what we are creates a despair that spurs us to change. We are obliged to try something else. In other words, the difference between what we want and what we are is the goad to dialectic.

Because our culture is besotted with commodity and entertainment, we are a culture in despair. Hegel put it this way: "Humanity is not at home with itself." (483) Despair is that feeling we have that we're living in a foreign culture even when we're in our own. It is the shame we feel when we think that our community itself behaves badly. Dropping uranium-hardened missiles on Iraqi cities, killing some citizens immediately and others over time due to radiation exposure, is not something of which any of us should be proud, never mind what our political representatives tell us. We know at some level that it cannot mean anything good to have political leaders such as George Bush, a man who has betrayed the public trust to the interests of corporations—and not furtively, but as an open, fundamental premise of his campaign. He is a man who, as of July 11, 2002, could advocate jail terms for corporate criminals accused of precisely the same corrupt accounting practices that he and Vice President Cheney were being investigated for (in Cheney's case with Haliburton, one of the firms implicated) and with exactly the same deceitful accounting firm, Arthur Andersen. (Where were the Republican Whitewater hounds of justice on Haliburton, by the way? Where the elaborate special counsels? Where the endless hours of vituperation on talk radio?)

With regard to foreign policy, it cannot mean anything good to be hated by so much of the rest of the world. And we're hated for good reason. Here's our lofty foreign policy in a nutshell: muck about the world "protecting our national interests," and when this mucking about blows back (as it has in Iran, Iraq, Afghanistan, Israel, and many other countries), return in overt indignation with B52s and cluster bombs. Bunker-busters. Stuff that bursts lungs and eardrums for miles. And it cannot mean anything good to live well at the expense of those who live in squalor. Once we get past Tiger Woods's beguiling smile, his entertaining style, and the lust for Buicks that he inspires, it cannot be good to have as a national "role model" a man who makes millions from a company like Nike that has the millions to give only because it is willing to run a global sweatshop. What Tiger Woods must represent for African Americans is bad enough, but what does he represent for his mother's people, the Thai, who along with other Asian people must live with the reality of these sweatshops? We might as well have Imelda Marcos for a role model.

If I'm wrong and facts like these don't cause us any national despair, I, for one, am willing to say that I despair over the absence of despair.

Fortunately, there are people capable of the work of context-building that we so desperately need. There are still people capable of thought. This critical project has been started for us in the work of George W. S. Trow, the author of *Within the Context of No Context* (1986) and *My Pilgrim's Progress* (1999). Before writing these books, Trow was a *New Yorker* staff writer for nearly thirty years. Trow's most recent book, *My Pilgrim's Progress*, is a work of social criticism whose real contribution to the genre (and, more importantly, to our situation) is a very persuasive ability to determine when a social formation is alive and dominant, and when it is dead. Trow's term for describing a social formation—appropriately, given our interest in the imagination—is "social aesthetic." For instance, he can tell us when the "Roosevelt aesthetic" was powerful and how and when it died.

I hate to try to simplify the thinking in *My Pilgrim's Progress*, because when it is good (and I think that most often it is superb), it is good "in the thickets." Trow is capable of taking us into the finest texture of a given historical "moment" and finding compelling symptoms of a more general dysfunction. For example, Trow provides a *tour de force*, improvisational close reading of the "theater" of a front page of the *New York Times* from February of 1950. It is the particularity and content that such close readings give his arguments that make his critique so forceful.

Nonetheless, it is possible to generalize. Trow argues that for the last fifty years the United States, at the height of its world dominance and authority, has been caught in a process of persistent social devolution that has left us with a world dominated by television and the likes of David Letterman. It is a world emptied of all honor and truthfulness, a world whose only depth is the abysmal depth of self-reflection and "ironic self-contempt." (Bless him, here, for not playing Harold Bloom and blaming it all on some vague thing called "postmodernism." Trow has too much intellectual self-respect for that demagogic gambit. He understands that if the present is bad, it is not a badness out of nothing and nowhere. Rather, this badness has been in process for a long time, cooking up through the culture.)

Trow presents his version of recent Western history as a movement of one dominant "aesthetic" into another. He begins with the Roosevelt aesthetic, the aesthetic into which he was born, and its dependence on the "country club" (i.e., extensive social networks of people who know, who have "information," and who know many others who know). It is the last moment of a certain kind of social integration, even if this integration is taking place at a very rarefied level of the social hierarchy.

Of course, this sort of presentation papers over a lot. It was, as Trow himself discusses later, a murderous hatred of the social privilege implied in this aesthetic that fueled the social rebellion of the sixties (witness Ginsberg's *Howl*). But the important thing for Trow is the *aesthetic*. In Trow's usage, the "aesthetic" is really a general proposition for how we all might choose to live together, and how we *do* live together in the moment in which a given aesthetic is powerful and dominant. Trow's point would seem to be, Never mind how flawed those old social aesthetics were (how dependent on small clusters of wealthy, privileged, and, yes, often cruel people), because things have only gotten worse since then, and it is instructive for us to look at what was good in them, poor dead things that they are.

Next came the Eisenhower aesthetic. As Trow says frequently, he "likes Ike." For Trow, Eisenhower was the last exemplar of a healthy, informed masculinity. (Unhappily, girls, it's a boy's life in Trow's world.) It's difficult at times to tell the difference between the Roosevelt and the Eisenhower aesthetics, but it seems that the crucial factor is the intervention of the Second World War and the consequent isolation of Eisenhower as the last man with enough information to make critical social decisions. He is the final end of the old patriarchal system, which sounds about right (and doesn't sound so unfortunate, even), except that, from Trow's perspective, it was also the end of a certain natural, honest decency far superior to what we have now in either our leaders or our culture in general. Roosevelt and Eisenhower were honest and decent in a way that Kennedy, Nixon, Reagan, and Clinton never could be.

The third moment to which Trow calls our attention is the moment of "vitalitarianism" (i.e., the cultural revolution of the 1960s), whose purpose was to overthrow the fraud of a life dominated by the "creeping catatonia" of television and the tabloid mind. Trow urges us to imagine Elvis in 1956 appearing for the first time on national television on the Tommy and Jimmy Dorsey Show. The incredible incongruity of it! Death of the past, birth of the future in that moment, crystallized, and on TV. The failure of this revolution of the "vitalitarians" (think Allen Ginsberg) was inherent in the fact that the only context for its energy was the very source of the problem it was trying to defeat: the media mind. Trow's moral is that a revolution for the good cannot happen in the "context of no information" (echoing the title of Trow's earlier book, *Within the Context of No Context*). But how *interesting* Trow's insight is that the sixties were not about the new or the mod, but about *nostalgia* for a lost authenticity, an authenticity which the citizens of that moment could not themselves ever have experienced, except intuitively. In this regard, Eisenhower and hippies are unlikely co-conspirators not only against the Military Industrial Complex but against Howdy Doody as well.

The final moment, which apparently began in 1997, if we are to take Trow's dates very literally, is the triumph of "ironic self-contempt." Here is the real suffering heart of the matter for Trow: Growing Up Damaged. This is the world of MTV, Jim Carrey, and David Letterman. His primary evidence is the "Cold Child," the child whose first mind is formed within the atmosphere of the Candace Bergen Sprint advertisements. Our moment, in the wake of the wreck of the sixties, is isolated, utterly lacking context, illiterate, illiberal, narcissistic, and empty of useful information. (Information is all for "exchange"; it's *money*, as our aptly titled Information Economy confesses.) That is our post-Reagan, Clinton-in-ascendance, cultural dominant. And damned if I can see good reasons why Trow is wrong to say so.

Trow's description of these three cultural moments is very persuasive, it seems to me, but I have a few reservations about his powerful critique. First, it is modernist in its tendency to look back for models of a more desirable sociality, in spite of the fact that Trow shows us repeatedly just how dead that past is. What is the *public* point of the powerful, emotional, fatherly attraction of Ike for Trow? How does this very informed nostalgia translate into a program for the *present?* Wasn't it exactly the attempt to recreate Eisenhower's fifties in Reaganism—but without the *information* and the social *context* that made Eisenhower's moment possible—that led to the social debacle (oh, a "prosperous" debacle it was, to be sure) of the eighties and nineties?

There is a second issue I'd like to take up. Where in this elaborate social history, this contextualizing of how we got to a place where we have no context, is the vantage-point from which the Trowist observes the fifty-year downward spiral of our cultural purpose? I find some troubling curiosities here. Trow frequently acknowledges the *New Yorker*, his longtime employer, the journal for which he was a journalist, but he never accounts for its social energies. Is the *New Yorker* part of the old pre-Roosevelt world of Brahmins and mavens? Isn't it dead, then? I don't mean to be picky here. My point is, when Trow worked for the *New Yorker*, was his perspective a *New Yorker* perspective? Everyone else in this book seems restricted to the determining particulars of his/her social context—even the mighty Eisenhower. Was Trow, as Byron said of Childe Harold, "among but not of" the *New Yorker* crowd? Is everybody in America a function of social aesthetics *except* George W. S. Trow? Or does he need to loosen the girdle on his account and allow for the possibility of, as I said of Mike Heppner, an ever-wayward, iconoclastic, reluctant (if not resistant), intellectually nomadic North American mind? No doubt, to find these eccentrics

Trow would have to look elsewhere than in the *New York Times* or mass media, something he seems ill prepared to do. (He's a *New Yorker*, stupid!) Maybe he'd even find an alternative hero to Eisenhower. (Gack. I'm sorry. I *am* persuaded by Trow's point of view, but Eisenhower! I can't go there.)

Another curiosity: the style of this book is not the formal, sincere, proper style of the old seriousness. It is not William Bennett. It is not even Paul Goodman. Trow's style is informal and gimmicky ("I'm going to rock-and-roll with this," he says). It is playful, odd in its juxtapositions, syntactically quirky, and full of rhetorical tics (that's the "Vonnegut of it," as Trow might say). In fact, this book often reads like a very good experimental novel of the *Tristram Shandy* variety, in which personal originality is a sure sign of virtue and you never meet a digression you don't like. And yet *My Pilgrim's Progress* is capable of many moments of great pathos and moral "sentence," as we used to say. In short, this book is—of all things—stylistically postmodern, and effectively so. It's Theodor Adorno meeting David Foster Wallace. Don't get me wrong: this is something I approve of! But isn't it strange that this old-school lover of decency and honesty and naturalness is dependent on a language which is impossible to imagine outside of the context of the last twenty years—exactly the period in which, by Trow's own account, we are most fallen? 'Tis passing strange!

Finally, I wonder how Trow thinks it possible that a book like this—such an admirable blend of intelligence, perception, independence, and deep caring—can be received in a moment so crippled by the problems Trow addresses: the media, television, celebrity, the gibberish of tabloids, the appealing nothingness that comes from the deep vacuum that is American life, culture, and thought in this year of our Lord 2003? Is this book itself not already "down the drain," as Trow likes to put it, a part of the dead past, and precisely because of its persistent intelligence? How can intelligence function in a period dominated by the cynical and profitable will-to-stupidity?

In the last analysis, Trow looks out on the world from an old, old precipice that he calls "liberal arts." He does admit that the liberal arts perspective is dead, or is part of a never-to-be-recuperated past. Nonetheless, in Trow's aesthetic, even "irrelevant people get to keep the sense of being they've traditionally had." In this fact is the pathos of what Trow has created: the intelligence and care that characterize his work are dead and irrelevant to the present "operating order" of social reality. To extend this problem to ourselves, Trow's readers, we might ask, "What does it mean, then, to read Trow and be convinced or persuaded by him—in short, to be persuaded by a social logic that you know from the outset to be without hope?" How depressing is that?

But for present purposes, let's confound the cultural dominant and allow the liberal arts view the last word. The liberal arts aesthetic, says Trow, is of and for a particular kind of person:

> And I don't mean just WASPs here. I mean Jews especially; people for whom books and book learning constituted not just a diversion, or a dominance reference, but a kind of prophetic factor in life. People for whom Thomas Hardy, on the one hand, or James Joyce, on the other, or both, if you were really smart and could make the connection, people for whom the best of the best constituted a kind of evolving bible of our American life. (39)

4.

My argument must now take a metaphysical turn because (I'll just be blunt about it) metaphysics understood in the way that I will encourage you to understand it is crucial to contending with the horrific social and ideological disaster we find ourselves confronted with. Worse yet, I need to argue, incorrigible yet ever hopeful artist and intellectual that I am, that Jacques Derrida's thought is an exemplary source of what it is that metaphysics has to offer us. Derrida can take us beyond the critical dead end of Trow's nostalgia for the liberal arts. Many will not like the sound of this proposition, but the unavoidable truth is that we can work metaphysics from our side, or we will be worked by it from the other side with consequences we won't enjoy. Is it not a plausible description of our cultural disaster that we are led by the nose by sinister ideological hacks of the kind I have surveyed in this book, but we refuse, as if there were a bad smell about it, the kind of thought that could save us?

There is a way of understanding metaphysics that is quite accessible, relevant, and important to my concerns in this book. Simply put, the essence of metaphysics is in the movement between the moment of criticism (in Derrida, *deconstruction*) and of reconstitution (in Derrida, *closure*). As Adorno writes in his posthumous book of lectures, *Metaphysics: Concept and Problems* (2001),

> [M]etaphysics is always present where enlightened rationalism both criticizes traditional notions and ideas, ideas existing in themselves, as mythological, and at the same time—and not just out of apologetic need, but out of a concern for truth—wants to save or restore these concepts, which reason has demolished, precisely through the application of reason, or even to produce them anew from within its own rational resources. (51)

Of utter importance here is the understanding that metaphysics understood as the relationship between critique and recuperation is not a doomed circle in which we are fated always to return to live what we know to be false. Rather, it is a commitment to metaphysics understood as how human beings learn to "think change." *The answer to the problem of the poverty of the imagination is simply that we must learn to think change.* Whether we call this capacity metaphysics or poetry or something else altogether is not as important as the presence of that force in the culture. But the models for thinking change that our history has given us are substantially philosophy and art. As William Carlos Williams wrote in *Kora in Hell,*

There is nothing sacred about literature, it is damned from one end to the other. There is nothing in literature but change and change is mockery. I'll write whatever I damn please whenever I damn please and as I damn please and it'll be good if the authentic spirit of change is on it. (13)

And it is here that American anti-intellectualism and American disdain for metaphysics seem most fatal. Because the only alternative to learning to think change is "faith," as our leaders like to put it, in our political process, in the honesty of our political representatives, in technology, and in the benign presence of capitalism. Nothing about the last few years of North American history gives me any reason to think that these things deserve our faith. Our political representatives and their parties have shown themselves to be venal, self-serving, obliged to corporations, and afraid of the collective strength of the military and the defense industry. To these people are trusted the authority over weapons that replicate the destructive power of stars. So, no question about it: We need to learn to think change. Then we need to *change*.

My sudden turn to metaphysics may seem abrupt and far afield from my interest in the imagination. But it is symptomatic of our present poverty that we think of art, philosophy, and the social as discrete and isolated. To my mind, the metaphysical movement between critique and reconstitution creates an ideal and fluid environment for the imagination and for art. The imagination takes advantage of the opportunities that critique creates in order to propose alternative human worlds—or it *should* do so, if it is healthy and not a mere vehicle for the maintenance of the status quo.

Whether or not we as a culture ever learn to think metaphysically, we are thought metaphysically every day. Aristotle's hylomorphic theory of composition—the division of matter and form, body and mind—thinks through us as the most commonsensical set of assumptions. Every day we think in Aristotle, whether we know it or not. Certainly, we have had philosophers such as Adorno and Derrida who have shown us very powerfully how to "think back" against the Aristotle-within. They have shown us that our Aristotelian conclusions are really problems, not certainties, and that these conclusions were problems for Aristotle as well. They have even shown how the philosophic procedure of discovering that conclusions are problems can have profound consequences for thinking about human society. But there remains an equally profound disconnect between what these philosophers have shown us and what we are willing and able to take up in our own turn as something with public consequence. I must confess that it is difficult for me not to think that this disconnect, this *failure*, says something fatal about the species.

All of which is to say, simply, that our culture lacks what is essential to philosophy and, I would argue, to spirituality: self-reflection. In the oldest Christian traditions, going back to St. Thomas and through him to Aristotle, God was pure self-reflection, the unmoved mover. When humans aspire to God, and seek to become properly (and literally) theo-logical, God-minded, they aspire to self-reflection. Thus the philosophy of Hegel is also a theology, because it describes a journey from the meanness of being "in itself" (all bare, explicit object, the world as a naked "given") to the most complete being "for itself" (and thus self-aware).

For Hegel, self-reflection is not a mere aping of God; it is God itself at work. Our consciousness is God's consciousness made concrete. It is God's consciousness at work in the world. According to Peter C. Hodgson, editor of Hegel's *Lectures on the Philosophy of Religion*, these lectures "issued in a project of world-transformation. Right-wing and left-wing impulses were held together in the center by a powerful vision of the God-world nexus." (24) This "God-world nexus," when fully realized, would produce what Hegel called, in a moment of naked optimism (but also a moment of intense human longing and faith) the "world in love." The world in love is the reconciliation of ethical thought with the real. Spiritual life, and thus God, is achieved when the concept of the ethical is realized concretely in the community. This is in marked contrast to political leaders who feel free to pay lip service to religious faith in a very abstract God while behaving like warmongers in the service of death merchants such as Lockheed-Martin in their everyday life. During those moments in history in which the world is in despair, we make the mistake of entrusting our self-understanding to self-interested liars, people for whom simple honesty is a threat. The parade of presidents, CEOs, and elected representatives pleading the Fifth Amendment in recent years would say that we have so entrusted our world; and the consequences for our self-understanding, for our community, for our spirit, and for our relation to a God principle are all as a consequence fatally threatened.

This lack of spiritual self-reflection, self-comprehension, and self-realization is both the need for imagination and the poverty of the imagination in the same moment. Incapable of self-reflection and openness to possibility, to "becoming," we sink into the Godlessness of mere assertion. We sink into great and bloody assertions of the Truth. In the place of philosophic honesty, we get lies "age old and age thick" from the Spielbergs, the public broadcasting gurus, the neo-cons like Harold Bloom, the economic planning "experts" like Florida, and, of course, at the top of the political food chain, our sometimes elected but in the fall of 2000 judicially selected president. Their lies are nothing less than a papering over of murder. They apologize for the knowing arrangement for suffering and torture in Indonesia, and Beirut, and El Salvador, and Afghanistan, and Iraq, and Cuba, and Palestine, and on and on.

And yet we continue to assume that our well-being is dependent on these "foreign" disasters. Inevitably, though, the effects of our well-oiled disaster machine will impinge upon us, too, whether as blow-back or as simple facts of the industrialized world. Consider the fact that while your grandmother's chances of getting breast cancer were one in twenty, your wife/daughter/sister's chances are one in eight. Or: we have the largest and most racist prison system in the world. For many communities here in Illinois, the prospect of a new prison is looked upon not as a community tragedy but as an opportunity for economic growth. The Richard Floridas of the world can celebrate the new Creative Age while the most common cause of death for black male teenagers remains homicide. Nothing about Florida's vision of the new economy has any real interest in changing such dismal facts of American life. That's a failure to imagine what's right around our own corner. Recall Wallace Stevens's words about the "pressure of reality" with which I began this book:

> In speaking of the pressure of reality, I am thinking of life in a state of violence, not physically violent, as yet, for us in America, but physically violent for millions of our friends and for still more millions of our enemies and spiritually violent, it may be said, for everyone alive. . . . A possible poet must be a poet capable of resisting or evading the pressure of the reality of this last degree, with the knowledge that the degree of today may become a deadlier degree tomorrow.

To which one might well respond, "Stop, will you? I couldn't live if I had to be conscious of these horrors at all times." To which Adorno responded, "Precisely." This is the meaning of his famous comment that after Auschwitz one cannot write poetry. Metaphysically, this extends to living itself. In the context of the world as organized violence—this failure that cannot be defeated—what right does anyone have to live? Isn't living well, being affluent, enjoying beauty an insult in the context of what Adorno called "the world of torture"? Even to indulge in metaphysics—the language of a certain hope, the form of thought that for Adorno was a "joy"—is an offense in this context, according to Adorno:

> Through Auschwitz—and by that I mean not only Auschwitz but the world of torture which has continued to exist after Auschwitz and of which we are receiving the most horrifying reports from Vietnam—through all this the concept of metaphysics has been changed to its innermost core. Those who continue to engage in old-style metaphysics, without concerning themselves with what has happened, keeping it at arm's

length and regarding it as beneath metaphysics, like everything merely earthly and human, thereby prove themselves inhuman. (101)

From Adorno's perspective, the meaning of the Information Economy is the final victory of the organization of "facts" over truth. The
brutal consequence of this victory is suffering and death for certain
"administered populations" and, at the best in the First World, a great
diminishment of what it means to be human. Demographics, population trends, market analyses, and gross national products replace truth.
To say that such a context is a bad place for artists says very little. It is
first the description of a general spiritual death. The "end of history"
that conservatives have celebrated becomes the end of hope for justice
and universal well-being. This is the vision of the world with which
Adorno confronts us.

What we need to do, to respond to Adorno's grim challenge, is
learn to recognize as an opportunity this awful dichotomy between suicide and living in guilt. Deconstruction would seize this binary and
recognize in it a gap, and it is in this in-between space that the imagination may risk its next gesture in inventing the idea of a world in
which one is not faced with such severe alternatives.

5.

Let me try to be more concrete about what consequences we might expect were our politics to become more "metaphysical." What are the
differences between living under the bromides and unexamined cant of
politicians and ideologists, and living under effective self-reflection?

In 2002, a collection of Jacques Derrida's essays on religion, Acts
of Religion, was published by Routledge. In this collection is an essay
titled "Faith and Knowledge: The Two Sources of 'Religion' at the
Limits of Reason Alone." This essay is very much in the style of Derrida's work of the last two decades. He is no longer doing primary

philosophical work in the development of concepts such as deconstruction; rather, he is discovering contexts such as literature, politics, friendship, and now religion in which the implications of his philosophical work can be seen and felt most concretely. I am not going to try to summarize Derrida's thought in this essay (which has a sometimes taxing, sometimes charming and rewarding drifting style, as always with the good Monsieur Derrida), but at the risk of doing violence to his work, I will go immediately to his primary deconstructive insight. It has much to say to us, especially to my concerns with war, technology, and globalism.

The common binary opposition that Derrida addresses in this essay, an opposition that is usually assumed without examination in the West as one of its basic assumptions, is the distinction between the sacred and the secular. The church and the state. Faith and reason. Derrida's astute (and deconstructive) observation is that the two are not separate, but are mutually dependent, and rightfully so. The violence of maintaining them as separate allows for certain mostly unfortunate acts in the name of politics and the state. In particular, in our War Against Terrorism, our guiding assumption is that all the "religion" is on the opposition side. Derrida's critical gesture makes that assumption very difficult to maintain, with dramatic consequences for our understanding of what it is that we are in fact doing.

Derrida describes two kinds of belief or faith. The first is the "faith"—the belief, credit, fiduciary trustworthiness, fidelity, confidence beyond all proof or demonstration—in our shared economic, legal, and political systems. This is ultimately a faith in founding principles organized around the ideas of justice and equality. The second form of faith is located in an experience of the holy or the sacred, that which is pure and uncontaminated by the worldly. Derrida's contention is that the distinction between the two forms of faith is a distinction without a difference. Both forms are "religious"; both are reflections of "spirituality."

What Derrida is appealing to in deconstructing this opposition between state and church is the fundamentally Hegelian insight that the constitution of ideas and values in the community is *spirit*. It is a serious expression of faith, a staking of one's life on principles, and it is utterly deserving of the name *religion*. "The fundamental concepts that often permit us to isolate or to *pretend* to isolate the *political*—restricting ourselves to this particular circumscription—remain religious or in any case theologico-political," argues Derrida. (63)

What must follow from this metaphysical insight is an acknowledgment that in our conflict with Islamic fundamentalists, the religious zeal is not all on their side. Our insistence in applying our notions of law and political process are historically rooted in religion, as Derrida reminds us:

> Wars or military "interventions," led by the Judaeo-Christian West in the name of the best causes (of international law, democracy, the sovereignty of peoples, of nations or of states, even of humanitarian imperatives), are they not also, from a certain side, wars of religion? (63)

This comes down to saying that if there is to be a global culture—and telecommunications and digital technology have made that appear inevitable (if also inevitably unequal)—that culture will be understood, rationalized, and administered in keeping with, in faith with, the "trust" we have in Western institutions. We simply do not know how to "trust" under other circumstances. It is a nearly imponderable dilemma; it is a *religious* dilemma, and a dilemma of spirit. How do we interact fairly with other people who do not share our faith in Western institutions? Unhappily, some perceive only one adequate response to it: the imposition of Western paradigms. This response is not in substance all that different from the classic colonialist imperative captured by Joseph Conrad's Kurtz in *The Heart of Darkness*: "Exterminate the brutes." We could perhaps now modify this to read, "Administer the brutes." But you can be sure that in the process of gaining the leverage to administer, we will also be obliged to exterminate some. Our war against al-Qaeda, however justified it may or may not be, is clearly a war of extermination. The CIA is on a sort of "pest" patrol with its armed drone aircraft.

The worldview that Derrida captures in his critique is not, to our disgrace, a mere caricature. In Dinesh D'Souza's *What's So Great About America* (2002), D'Souza does us the favor of being straightforward about the process of resurrecting not merely the rhetoric of colonialism but that of the Crusades (for in fact George II spoke very truthfully when he used the word "crusade" in those first dark moments post–9-11). For D'Souza, the Muslim world is "inferior" and a "failure." Islam needs to change "in order to survive and flourish in the modern world" (i.e., in a world dominated by Western political and financial models). (186) The United States, on the other hand—established upon Christianity, capitalism, and democracy—is "a new kind of society that produces a new kind of human being. That human being—confident, self-reliant, tolerant, generous, future oriented—is a vast improvement over the wretched, servile, fatalistic and intolerant human being that traditional societies have always produced, and that Islamic societies produce now." (192–93) For D'Souza it is a matter of "some cultures are advanced and others are backwards." (40) Sounds simple enough.

America is, in short, D'Souza writes (quoting Abraham Lincoln), "the last best hope for the world." (193) D'Souza's recommendations for realizing this hope are two, and so far as I can see they are indistinguishable from the logic of colonialism's "white man's burden."[4] First, "we need to destroy their terrorist camps and networks." (184) Although

---

[4] To be sure, this is not the first time that D'Souza has been accused of being an apologist for colonialism, to which charge he responds, in this book, "Nonsense." After all, colonialism is a bad thing, and the good Dinesh would not knowingly be associated with a bad thing. His explanation is essentially that while Western colonialism was a bad thing done for bad reasons, it nonetheless had many good consequences, not the least of which is the fact that most of the colonized countries have remained institutionally European even after the end of colonialism. This is an incomplete Hegelian thought. For Hegel, the history leading to the absolute was a "slaughter bench." Bad things happened but good things came of them. But this did not mean, for Hegel, that we should say, "Hurrah for the slaughter bench." The problem with D'Souza's argument is not that it apologizes for the past, but that it projects those same bloody procedures into the future as if they were our best hope.

D'Souza spends exactly no time describing what this blandly stated "destruction" will require, and at what cost to ourselves and civilian populations around the world, this recommendation implies an enormous and probably futile military campaign on multiple continents. Terrorists are guerrilla fighters on a global field. If you thought eradicating the activities on the Ho Chi Minh trail was frustrating, what will it mean to eliminate activities in Chechnya, the Philippines, Sudan, Switzerland, and on and on? It will take more than laser-guided technology.

Next, and even more controversially, we need "to turn Muslim fundamentalists into classical liberals." (184) "This does not mean that we want them to stop being Muslims," D'Souza says. "It does mean, however, that we want them to practice their religion *in the liberal way*." (185, italics mine) Just why can't those nasty Arabic Muslims be European Muslims? Think about it. Wouldn't a cup of espresso and a brioche help with all that bowing and scraping toward Mecca? A little pick-me-up is nice for all God's children.

Derrida's more serious response to D'Souza's claim would be that you cannot glibly separate out our Latinate legal structures from our religious beliefs, and you cannot imagine that by obliging Muslims to live by this worldview you are not doing violence to their religion. To his credit, D'Souza acknowledges this in stark terms:

> Our newest challenge comes from a very old adversary. The West has been battling Islam for more than a thousand years. It is possible that this great battle has now been resumed, and that over time we will come to see the seventy-year battle against communism as a short detour. (187)

In short, we must pick up the long-fallen battle flag of the Great Crusade and once again send our children to fight, protected this time not by divine puissance but by their own Nintendo-hardened reflexes. The infidel will bow to the name of our faith. Which is to say, he will bow to technology, the final meaning of our superiority. Technology, for D'Souza, is the luminous offspring of the "marriage between science and capitalism." (66) Technology is our virtue and our might. But it is terribly significant that D'Souza and the conservative establishment are willing to acknowledge that our war with Islam is not a war with some arbitrary evil, a blast from the happenstansical blue, but a war with crimes and criminals (for indeed they are criminals every bit as much as our presidents and secretaries of state have been international criminals for the last three decades) that must be seen in a global and historical context. For D'Souza's concessions about this war as a holy war will be deeply troubling even for those Americans to whom CNN has the EZ-poll hotline hardwired to the frontal lobe. D'Souza's convictions about our faith confirm Derrida's suspicions. D'Souza:

> To believe in the Greek notion of a reality that is not arbitrary, that obeys mathematical laws, a reality that is reasonable and susceptible to human understanding, is to have a certain kind of faith—a faith in reason. (62)

So, our new crusade will be an Enlightenment Crusade based not on revelation but on reason. This is a crusade after the death of God. Still, I'd like to see the public discourse surrounding our military and economic activities in the Middle East proceed from the question of whether or not it should be our national purpose to succeed where the original Crusades failed. Can the Bushites muster a majority for such a prospect? That debate would at least mark an improvement in public discourse over our obsession with "evildoers." It will not, however, be any less disturbing.

The metaphysical moment of deconstruction's critique is an act of imagination. The imagination works in the assumption of a lack in the present reality. The imagination is messianic. It anticipates the coming of something other than the irreducibility of what-we-have. The imagination is a desiring machine. It expresses a desire to realize the Enlightenment promise of justice, freedom, and creativity. As Derrida points out, profoundly, these terms are ultimately *mystical*.

We work in their name without knowing exactly what they mean, let alone what they could be. Nonetheless, they are still critical, as Derrida reminds us:

> Nothing seems to me less outdated than the classical emancipatory ideal. One cannot attempt to disqualify it today, whether crudely or with sophistication, without at least some thoughtlessness and without forming the worst complicities. It is true that it is also necessary to re-elaborate, without renouncing, the concept of emancipation, enfranchisement, or liberation. . . . (258)

All the calculation and negotiation of law has as its final purpose the creation of a representation of the promise of these ultimately incalculable terms. The imagination, in its turn, must continue to say, "That's not it. Not it at all. A periphrastic study in a worn-out poetical fashion [as Eliot put it in the *Four Quartets*]. Let's try again." And then, "What about this? It is perhaps something we could call beautiful. Does it present a world you could choose to live in?"

The imagination aspires to Derrida's vision of deconstruction:

> [Deconstruction would like] not to remain enclosed in purely speculative, theoretical, academic discourses but rather . . . to aspire to something more consequential, to *change* things and to intervene in an efficient and responsible [way], not only in the profession but in what one calls the city, the *pólis*, and more generally the world. Not to change things in the no doubt rather naive sense of calculated, deliberate and strategically controlled intervention, but in the sense of *maximum intensification of a transformation in progress*. . . . (236, italics mine)

Deconstruction is a "privileged instability," and the gap it opens is the imagination's spiritual home.

6.

I suppose it goes without saying that the species of religion I have been describing here, cobbling together Hegel's idea of spirit with Derrida's notion of the mystical, is nothing like what is commonly construed as religion. And the idea that religion needs "imagination" will strike most nominally religious people in this country as bizarre if not blasphemous. Religion is about *conviction,* in the full, cruel ambiguity of that term. And yet I would contend that what's most wrong with religion (especially American-style Christianity) is that its imagination is debased.

Consider the tales we receive from certain Christian writers. In Ed Murphy's *The Handbook for Spiritual Warfare,* Murphy tells a story of being summoned home by his wife because his daughter is possessed by a demon. She's a teenager. She's talking back. Getting angry. Listening to heavy metal. I know it sounds like adolescence, but in fact it's Satan. Finally, the daughter confesses that a boy gave her a pentagram to wear around her neck (to intensify that AC/DC spawn-of-Satan groove). The demon is promptly dispatched by the father, who regains his proper authority over all things daughterly. When he's not busy ridding daughters of the heavy metal demon, he's reviving the old war against masturbation (a word which, he fears, will cause his reader such distress and shame that he sometimes calls it "autosexuality"):[5]

> Bondage to masturbation is spiritual warfare. The desire may first come from within, warfare with the lusts of the flesh. It can also come directly from without, warfare with a sex-crazed world. Finally, it often comes from above, warfare with sexual demons who tempt us to unwise or illicit sexual activity. (151)

To be fair, intellectually vulgar books like *The Handbook for Spiritual Warfare* are perhaps among the least subtle contemporary works on

---

[5] Oh, you mean the old rattlesnake shake!

Christianity. But they are in every Christian bookstore and every Borders and Barnes & Noble, and they sell hundreds of thousands if not millions of copies. For example, Bruce Wilkinson's *The Prayer of Jabez* has turned religious publisher Multnomah Press into a multi-million-dollar success story. *The Prayer of Jabez* has sold 9.3 million copies (plus the copy I unhappily bought). Wilkinson's books boosted the company's revenues from $30 million to $50 million last year. *The Prayer of Jabez* is surely not as vulgar as Murphy's *Handbook,* and it doesn't ask us to be "warriors," thank goodness. Its argument has mainly to do with asking God to enlarge the individual's capacity for doing God's work. Still, simple narratives about confronting Satan or the Antichrist are the foundation of the book. Wilkinson provides the following dialogue:

> "What can I do for you?" I asked.
> "I'm afraid of the Antichrist," she replied. "For fifty years, I've lived in dread that I won't recognize him when he comes and that I'll be deceived by him and receive the mark of the beast." (42)

However much we might want to excuse individuals for the childish naiveté required to take such narratives literally, as a symptom of a social state of affairs these narratives are incontestably real and incontestably impoverishing. Which isn't, however, to say that they aren't powerful. Such narratives are part and parcel of the self-righteous rhetoric that provides justification for many of our most egregious political acts, as when, in 2002, the Bush administration withdrew American support for UN-sponsored family planning because some aspect of that program suggested support for abortion.[6]

---

[6]Why it is, exactly, that God prefers the deaths by starvation of living children to the abortion of unborn children is not explained. Thirty-five thousand children starve to death every day in the most overpopulated and impoverished countries of our world. Meanwhile, the religious right maintains its political alliance with a global capitalism determined to ensure that poor countries and their children stay poor. They do it the old-fashioned way: they exploit them.

And yet there are many worthy historical premises for religion that can seem only heretical in the insufferably sanctimonious present. William Blake wrote, "A man must invent his own religion or be enslaved by another's." Was there any difference at all between the imagination and religion for Blake? Even the Christianities of Dante, or Chaucer, or Gerard Manley Hopkins, orthodox though they were in many ways, were first profoundly consonant works of the imagination. Without the art that made their works idiosyncratic, the religious substance of their works would fail. Or consider Sören Kierkegaard, a person for whom no faith was worthy of the name that didn't begin in doubt. He had to entirely reconceive, elaborately and inventively, the story of Abraham and Isaac in his great work *Fear and Trembling* simply in order to provide a place where he could stand in faith's light in good conscience. But in what sense, the faithful might ask, is Kierkegaard's heretical recasting of the story of Abraham and Isaac a part of God's word? For Kierkegaard, as for Hegel, the Bible is the beginning not the end of a human dialogue that is without necessary end. If we are sensitive to Hegel's God/world nexus, religious thought thinks through us and with us as necessary collaborators. It does not merely inform us didactically.

Of course, to stand before Christian faith as it is typically articulated in the present is plainly not to stand before the faith that Blake and Kierkegaard understood. Most popular articulations of Christian faith are all too self-certain of their superiority to the world's "garbage religions." As Dinesh D'Souza put it, Islam produces "wretched, servile, fatalistic, intolerant" humans. As spiritual people, we have shut down our capacity not only for compassion but for any real imaginative understanding of any faith, our own included. As Viktor Shklovsky, in *The Third Factory*, wrote of the social imagination in Stalinist Russia:

> An oyster draws the valves of its shell together with a supreme effort. Having drawn them shut, it stops functioning. Its muscles no longer radiate heat, but they do hold the valves shut.

Prose and poetry are being held shut in such a death grip. Muscles warm and living could never exert the necessary force.

Thirty-three-year-old shell, I am sick today. I know how heavy is the force that keeps the valves together. That should not be. (25)

Shklovsky's words could be applied to every aspect of the impoverished imagination that I have spoken of in this book. Its relevance to popular religious thought is particularly sobering.

Chapter 5

NOTES TOWARD THE NEXT AMERICAN SUBLIME

And the sublime comes down
To the spirit itself,
The spirit and space,
The empty spirit
In vacant space.
What wine does one drink?
What bread does one eat?

> Wallace Stevens,
> "The American Sublime"

The strong assumption in the contemporary academy is that the idea of beauty is disreputable. Disgraced. No person of conscience speaks of it. It has been banished from the conversation. Literature is not about art; it's about privilege and the politics of representation. Does this not create the weird spectacle of a scholarship condemning and banishing exactly that thing that it had come to the table to discuss? This is like astronomers deciding that they're done accounting for the stars. Henceforth, astronomers will concern themselves only with what people have said about the stars. Or, even more apropos, what has been said about the stars in pop songs. As a consequence, beauty does not exist in our academies of higher learning. As we've seen, it's only worse in the happy world of the Middle Mind, where everything is beautiful, even the banal.

Against these currents I have tried to present an understanding of the imagination and art that is both deeply committed to and formally involved with historical time but that is at the same time urgently engaged in the possibility of change. Through the work of the imagination, beauty is how we learn to think change while remaining faithful to specific traditions of human creativity.

But the turn I made in the last chapter toward an understanding of art's relationship to spirit and the mystical cannot be entirely accounted for by the idea of beauty. For this turn we need the sublime. It is here that the imagination will be most forceful, most positive, and most ambitious. It will also be most hopeful. This version of the imagination will be sublime precisely where it engages artistically what Derrida describes as the "mystical" aspect of our social thinking. When we speak of justice, freedom, or creativity, we do not know entirely what we mean. These are not calculable concepts, and yet they are the entire force behind what we claim we want in the human world.

We are told, of course, that we already have all of the justice, freedom, and creativity we have any right to expect in our Western, neoliberal, free-market democracies. We are told this with the sort of intensity that reveals the fear of the consequences if this claim were ever shown to be false. The truth is that this claim is the Big Lie. It's like life in an alcoholic family, where all the family members are daily obliged to reaffirm that everything is whole and right and normal. But inside the children are saying, "Oh, I feel this big pain that I can't explain. I must say what isn't, and yet I can't say what I need to say. So frightening is the prospect of saying what can't be said that I'm afraid even to *think* what can't be said. And so I'm afraid even to think at all." Every day our social imagination is asked to defile itself by confirming a lie. And every day most of us run from the horror of confirming a lie by refusing to think.

What waits beyond the lie is the sublime. For Kant, the sublime was both pleasure and pain. The pleasure of recognition and the pain of inaccessibility. For the imagination to take up the cause of the sublime again will release us from the despair of the Big Lie. It will open up to us the pleasure of trying to reinvent and make present the ideas of justice, freedom, and creativity. But it will also labor under the necessary disappointment that, however artful its inventions, it never quite gets to "It." As Jean-François Lyotard writes, describing Kant:

[The sublime] takes place, on the contrary, when the imagination fails to present an object which might, if only in principle, come to match a concept. We have the Idea of the World (the totality of what it is), but we do not have the capacity to show an example of it. (136)

Or as Adorno puts it in *Aesthetic Theory*, as always more pithily,

Art desires what has not yet been, though everything that art is has already been. It cannot escape the shadow of the past. (134)

In spite of the fact that the imagination cannot finally make its sublime object fully present, the mere idea that it is trying strikes terror into the heart of dominant assumptions. One way of thinking about the work of Steven Spielberg and the many others I have surveyed here, the panoply of strategies in the Middle Mind in particular, is that they are preemptive efforts to saturate the field in which the imagination might do its work. This is the frenzy of communication, of information. This is the televisual deluge. This is communication as domination. We drown at the bottom of Hollywood's ocean, and all we ever wanted was a single glass of pure water.

The Next American Sublime, as I am imagining it, would not seek merely to say the unsayable. Its function would not be solely theological. It would also be pragmatic (as befits an *American* sublime). This is a sublime for the here-and-now. This is a sublime of finite things. We will be in its aura when it creates a yearning for something on the other side of what we have. The sublime beckons. We can hear it breathing on the other side of the brutal actuality of the world. It will suggest something without being able to say it, but just that willingness to suggest will make it disruptive, disturbing, destabilizing, and dangerous.

But just what can it mean, this "pragmatic sublime"? It is, after all, a queer bundle of terms that I am gathering under the idea of the social imagination: it is mystical, sublime, and somehow pragmatic to boot. But it may also be just exactly what we need in these dogmatic and authoritarian times. Louis Menand's superb book *The Metaphysical Club: A Story of Ideas in America* provides a rich account of the consequences of the intellectual discoveries of Oliver Wendell Holmes, William James, Charles Peirce, and John Dewey gathered under the rubric of American "pragmatism." His account reveals that the pragmatic has always been at heart sublime. That is, pragmatism has been a method committed to making concrete things which it only distantly understood. Menand's book reminds us that there are in fact certain core ideas in pragmatism that help to illuminate why the sublime, as I am using that term, can be pragmatic:

- Philosophy is not about truth.

- All knowledge is social.

- When we assert a claim about the world and act on it, we change the nature of the world.

But when pragmatism "asserts a claim," this claim is not based on some indisputable concrete Truth. Rather, it is based on a desire. It is an intuition about the Good. It is mystical, in Derrida's term, and it is sublime. As Menand writes, "Knowledge is not a passive mirroring of the world, but an active means of making the world into the kind of world we want it to be." (225) The notion of the sublime as I have been using that term is the assertion of a belief in things (freedom, justice, creativity) that we could not give an adequate empirical account of—in other words, that are not True—but that nonetheless provide the premises for the force of our activities in the world.

Art is thus most pragmatic, and most consequential for the social, when it is most sublime, when it asserts its intuitions about what it means to be free, just, or creative. Art is most properly useful when it doesn't know exactly what it is about. It is most real when it is merely following its nose. That the artistic imagination must do its work formally, through invention, and not through self-certain didacticism, or "meaning," is art's way of confessing that it doesn't know quite what it means but that it is willing to assert its claim on the future anyway. It is also in this way that art wishes to have its social consequences. Thus, the imagination joins pragmatism in "betting."

As Menand puts it, "Beliefs are just bets on the future." (440) The pragmatist's wager is the ongoing Enlightenment version of Pascal's divine wager (I believe in God because I have nothing to lose if he doesn't exist, and much to gain if he does). It is through this "wager" that pragmatism asserts a desire that thought, whether philosophic or artistic, should be of immediate use to the world. Menand quotes Thomas Dewey: "Philosophy recovers itself when it ceases to be a device for dealing with the problems of philosophers and becomes a method, cultivated by philosophers, for dealing with the problems of men." (362) Dewey wanted "to get the social organism thinking." It is unhappily the case that, in its present damaged condition, the public mostly has contempt for thought, certainly for European thought, but even for the thought of Dewey and the American pragmatists who provided the intellectual basis for basic modern democratic assumptions such as universal suffrage, equal rights before the law, and freedom of speech, especially in academic contexts. As Menand points out, Justice Oliver Wendell Holmes helped to ground these values in legal precedents that to this day function to protect us from the logic of premodern thinking such as that of the 1857 Dred Scott decision. In Dred Scott, the United States Supreme Court argued, "The black man has no rights that a white man is bound to respect." In the present, a similar mentality might say that no foreign culture has rights that the march of capital and military superiority is obliged to respect. Hence, the McDonaldization of the globe, or, worse yet, the Lockheed-Martinizing of the globe.[1] But where is the opportunity in our own

---

[1] *New York Times* columnist Thomas Friedman claims that economy and military are in fact the same thing. McDonald's cannot flourish without McDonnell Douglas. He writes, "The hidden hand of the market will never work without the hidden fist."

culture for the kind of thought that might "wager against" this ruling logic? Where is our Holmes? In the Middle Mind? In the Rehnquist Supreme Court, where justices like Anthony Scalia gloat about the court's role in defrauding the people of Florida of their democratic will?

Derrida poignantly echoes Dewey's desire for a return of thought to the social when he claims that deconstruction aspires "to *change* things . . . in the sense of maximum intensification of a transformation in progress." (*Religion,* 236) This vaguely worded "transformation in progress" is loaded with Derrida's idea of the "mystical." We place a wager on the future and we throw ourselves into winning, just as Oliver Wendell Holmes threw himself into the Civil War in the idea that slavery should not be part of the future and that social equality should mean something real. We bet that freedom and justice are the most deserving human beliefs, and we press that conviction socially and historically.

The concept of human freedom is something we ourselves have invented as a "good," and we have made historical commitments to this notion with our lives. We have "wagered" on it. In fact, this idea matters only because we have staked our lives on it through our historical acts, some of which have been those acts we call art. This call to "freedom" is a dangerous gambit, to be sure, and full of the uncertainties that Derrida has called mystical. What does it mean to be "free" after all? What does it mean to be "fully alive"? These concepts do not yield to any concrete calculus. Nevertheless, like Derrida, Theodor Adorno signaled his final solidarity with the frustrated purposes of the Enlightenment concept of human freedom and capacity when he wrote, in *Metaphysics,*

> You may think me an old-fashioned Enlightenment thinker, but I am deeply convinced that there is no human being, not even the most wretched, who has not a potential which, by conventional bourgeois standards, is comparable to genius. (132–33)

Oddly enough, it is art, in all its inarticulateness, that best understands the difficulties of our collective social wagers, and best intuits what these abstractions can and should mean. Art and the imagination lead us away from communication as domination, away from mere communication's impoverishing of the imagination, away from "information," and toward an intuition about our activities as the feeling of being alive.

This pragmatic/sublime understanding of art and the imagination is conspicuously not art as cultural shrine, government-sanctioned museum, or canon. It is not the *product* of artistic making—something that can be hung on the wall or sold at Barnes & Noble—that is the point for either artist or audience. The point is the process of discovering the freedom of human invention. Gilbert Sorrentino, one of our greatest writers and thinkers, puts it this way:

> The finished work is, for its maker, a kind of intrusion into his life, almost an affront to it. It marks a full stop and guarantees nothing but that which is self-evident: that his work is over. What is most disturbing to him, as I have suggested, is that this completion does not presage anything in the way of future work. The well-known state called "writer's block," and the equally frustrating state in which the writer writes, but writes badly, are bitter and destructive, not because they obtrude between the writer and the finished product, but because they cut him off from the process of creation itself, that process which tells him that he is alive. (5)

The so-called "audience" (which the Middle Mind would have us think of as mere "consumers") takes up the intuitions of the artist in its turn. The imagination says, "Life is this way," and we follow. This makes art dangerous to the dictatorship of the present. This is how art and the imagination begin to have a strong social presence.

For instance (although this is not an American instance), Federico Fellini's *Amarcord* is a movie about Italy during the reign of Mussolini's fascism. This was a dark and painful period for Italy, and the mark of that darkness is everywhere in the movie. And yet the movie is mostly gentle and comic. It does not overtly condemn fascism or its brutality, and any remedy it offers is not a literal social or political proposition. *Amarcord*'s humor, visual richness, inspired juxtapositions and movements between narrative elements, and huge sense of human eros all work together to create a longing, but it is not a longing for any particular political paradigm. No ideology. No answers. Rather, Fellini creates a desire to live in his created world that is so much less an achieved world than the world Mussolini created. It is Fellini-world. You want to live in its gentle, humane, comic, erotic ethos. Fellini creates social longing for something we don't have (and that Italy certainly didn't have during the era of fascism), and this longing brings with it a subtle but serious impatience not only with the safely dead dictators of the past but with the dictators of the moment.

The most ambitious filmmaker of the American sublime is David Lynch, most successfully in *Blue Velvet*. Lynch is sublime in part because he is inarticulate. He really has no idea what he's trying to say. He's at his best when he keeps speaking anyway, trusting to his always shocking intuitions. He's at his worst when he determines to "explain," as he has done too often in his work since *Blue Velvet*.

Blue Velvet is a famously "disturbing" film. It is offensive to "puritans of all stripes," as Adorno put it. It is disturbing because it neither condemns nor condones the multifold malice it depicts. Violence, drug abuse, madness, sexual cruelty. It is disturbing because, through the character of Jeffrey Beaumont (played by Kyle MacLachlan), Lynch seems to suggest that we ourselves are ambivalent about the evil represented by Frank Booth (Dennis Hopper). Frank's evil is both attractive and repulsive. (As Frank says to Jeffrey, "You're like me.") Frank is like Satan in Milton's *Paradise Lost*: he has all of the work's charisma and certainly the majority of its good lines. The film comes to life when Frank enters. Given what I earlier identified as Hollywood's super-aesthetics of violence and empty sexual display (something Lynch himself has been guilty of),[2] there is good reason to think that Americans, in particular, are ambivalent about this evil. Our culture would seem to insist that all official pronouncements condemn it, and yet we daily indulge in it. *Blue Velvet* makes this ambiguity in our national character unavoidable and thus uncomfortable.

There is no simple opposition to the evil we find, with Lynch, on the other side of a dismembered ear, at the end of a long tunnel where music sounds like the thrum of dark blood, there among the milling bugs. The only explicit gesture toward the Good that Lynch allows is the cloying vision of Sandy Williams (Laura Dern). With church organs oozing in the background, Sandy says, "Thousands of robins flew down and they brought this blinding light of love." But this robin, perched on the windowsill at the movie's end, is too fake. This is such a stilted, bathetic, and altogether false robin that its promise is revoked in laughter in the instant it is introduced. The fake robin is a way for Lynch to say, "I don't know how to express what stands opposed to Frank. But I have the unhappy duty to tell you that it is not robins, not beautiful tulips before a white picket fence, and not the red reassurance of a fire truck with a Dalmatian. I won't lie to you."

What is critical to understand is that the fraudulence of Sandy's vision of robins—famous bug-eaters—is not an indication of hopelessness or moral capitulation to Frank's world. It's true that Lynch does not and probably cannot articulate an ethical/political "position" in opposition to Frank. He cannot create a literal politic. Lynch's notion of the Good is inarticulate. It is sublime. If it is to be found anywhere, it is in the formal art of the movie itself. That is his "objective correlative"

---

[2] The lesbian love scenes in *Mulholland Drive* and Laura Palmer's repeatedly displayed breasts in *Fire Walk with Me* are nothing more than Hollywood striptease and naked (so to speak) pandering to trite expectation. Consider, in contrast, Isabella Rossellini's Dorothy Valens walking naked, bleeding, and brutalized toward Jeffrey at *Blue Velvet*'s climax. She is anything but titillating. She captures the horror and the moral authority of the famous photograph of a napalmed Vietnamese girl. (In an interview in the *Blue Velvet* documentary *Mysteries of Love*, Rossellini claims she consciously tried to imitate the girl's posture.)

for the Good. Frank's evil (and America's violent sexual demons) is confronted most effectively by David Lynch's style, his cinematic voice. His style does not appease or indulge Frank's chaos. It is not a style that says, as Frank says, "I'll fuck anything that moves." Rather, Lynch's style is elegant and carefully framed. *Blue Velvet's* visual style seems almost impatient with the plot. In a splendid moment of loving illogic early in the film, the camera interrupts the growing police melodrama in order to consider a man standing bowlegged in front of a gift store while he plays with a key chain. This brief but utterly irrelevant shot says no to Frank's world. Such moments in Lynch are intuitive but perfect. In *Blue Velvet*, Frank's evil is mastered by Lynch's art. How unlike our official world this is! In our official world, crime is confronted by pious religious posturing and more violence, whether directed at drug dealers or foreign rulers in need of a "regime change."

Most American cinema, even "artsy" movies like *American Beauty*, lack the courage and artistic capacity to trust to this formal sublime (although the *possibility* of the sublime is present in *American Beauty* in a dreamlike and windblown plastic bag that recurs repeatedly throughout the film). In the absence of any real commitment to its materials, *American Beauty* must retreat to fixed and familiar political "positions." In the end, the film reconfirms what it had seemed to be attacking: the essential, final goodness of the family, in spite of it all. After all of its charades at revolt, *American Beauty* is finally a family values movie. Its abstracted "meaning" (and brother does it have one) is perfectly appropriate for the Christian Broadcasting Network, even if some of the film's material is not.

When the character of Lester Burnham (Kevin Spacey) stares into the photograph of his family in his dying moments, the viewer is either ideologically comforted or defrauded. This viewer, at least, understood at that moment that the movie had not been serious about either the drama of social revolt (Lester's running amok, quitting his job, taking drugs, doing his own thing) or the potential of artistic vision (in the blowing bag). *American Beauty* betrays the imagination. The last-minute affirmation of the nuclear family is the equivalent of a deathbed conversion to the church true and righteous of conventional morality, and all the darkness and doubt preceding it is revealed, in hindsight, as a fashionable pretense. So anxious is director Sam Mendes to please that he not only confirms the conservative ethos of family values but also confirms the emerging liberal morality against homophobia with the same gesture (the fateful murder at the movie's end, committed by a deranged and homophobic military man who imagines, wrongly, that Lester is gay). You'd think Mendes was running for Congress, so desperate is he to accommodate all political positions.[3] The film pretends to the radicalism of refusal of the status quo, throws a gay rights bone to liberals, but is finally deeply conservative.

Consider, in contrast, the exemplary work of Japanese filmmaker "Beat" Takeshi Kitano. Kitano's "yakusa" gangster films are able to reveal in stunning moments of visual beauty that in spite of the violence of his films Kitano understands and desires the sublime and intuitive world of life, creativity, and play. For example, in *Brother* (2001) two gangsters stand on top of a Los Angeles office building and send a paper airplane sailing down to the street below. The camera patiently follows the long, slow, looping descent of the plane. Hollywood assumptions would argue that such a scene was irrelevant, tedious, and a distraction from the real purpose of the movie: violence (also known as "entertainment"). The tragedy of Kitano's vision is that this appeal to the sublime must take place in a world committed full-force to death.

Similarly, in *Blue Velvet*, David Lynch provides no false comforts. It is the stunningly strange visual and musical and narrative montage

---

[3] It is not surprising that this film is finally conventional. *American Beauty* is of and for the world of the Middle Mind. The film is a Steven Spielberg DreamWorks production, and the screenplay was written by Alan Ball (interviewed by Terry Gross in relation to HBO's *Six Feet Under*). *American Beauty* also confirms the expectations of the two super-aesthetics of American cinema: violence and striptease. Lester's brains are blown enamel-red against a white wall as if it were an abstract expressionist painting, and there are no fewer than two stripteases by the film's youngest actresses, one of whom strips at a window as her voyeur boyfriend videotapes the scene from his house next door.

of the film that produces an intuition of an imagined wholeness, a wholeness of and by the imagination; and imagined wholeness is Lynch's only real opposition to evil. It is not that one would choose to live in the world Lynch depicts (never mind that it's more like the world we do live in than we'd care to admit), but that one would choose to live in a world with the freshness of intuition and the moral integrity of the artwork *Blue Velvet*. The formal character of the art carries all the virtue.

While *Blue Velvet* provides a way of anticipating the Next American Sublime, it hardly provides a concrete example of creating social change in its own moment. Firmly lodged in the Reagan eighties, Lynch's radical potential was isolated and suspended like an insect in dark amber. It had little opportunity to dialogue with other social forces, as movies such as Costa-Garvas's Z and even apparently apolitical films such as Fellini's *Satyricon* did in the high sixties. Which is to say that art and the imagination cannot be "pragmatic," and cannot have the social effect they seek in a climate that is generally repressive. When the Middle Mind turns art into entertainment, when academia turns art into sociology, when conservatives turn art into museum pieces or canon-fodder, and when the only imagination with broad credibility is one in which technology is presented as destiny, the resulting context is barren—*impoverished*—for art and the imagination. We might say that such elaborate countermeasures are testimony to art's intrinsic potential for power—for what Adorno called "social explosiveness" and what Stevens called "poetry as a destructive force." But such testimony does little to contradict the fact that at present the social imagination is very much depressed.

In contrast, at its best, much of the popular art of the sixties was a very effective art of the pragmatic sublime. The compelling surreal poetry of Bob Dylan's "Visions of Johanna" has had more enduring political force than the earlier overt old-left politics of songs like "Only a Pawn in Their Game." And the shocking pop art of the cover of *Sgt. Pepper's Lonely Hearts Club Band* made a broad public appeal to a "beyond." (Adorno in *Aesthetic Theory*: "Works become beautiful by the force of their opposition to what simply exists." [51]) These works of the sixties argued quite plainly, as the imagination will, that the world doesn't have to be the way it is, that change is real, and that the future is to be imagined. The art of that moment was fortunate to have a social context capable of taking up its challenge and responding provocatively so that artists, in their turn, could ratchet up the stakes yet again. Of course, and I suppose it goes without saying, there was also much up-against-the-wall stupidity in the art and politics of the sixties, and I think that stupidity finally overwhelmed the more subtle provocations of Dylan and others. Finally, the social climate of the sixties was not capable of taking up the sublime as its ethos. That social space has yet to arrive.

And so the greatest practical desire of the imagination, caught in its present Middle-Minded Slough of Despond, must be to be taken up once again by its own society. As I've said, this happened in a limited and incomplete way in the 1960s, but even in this limited and incomplete form it had a tremendous impact on the future. For good and bad, the imagination was "at large" in the sixties in a way it is not in the present. It was out and about, a dangerous vagabond, a Pied Piper. But the imagination is presently "institutionalized" in universities and museums and the inane cultural programming of the media, as if we feared having something so mad walking the streets. In the present, the only "thought" that is completely and actively socialized is *fear*. What else was the midyear national election of 2002 about? In the end, as the imagination could tell us if we'd let it, this fear is self-defeating, because it commits us to the worst things our culture is capable of. We fear ourselves, especially dark-skinned males among us, so we need guns in our homes, never mind who those guns will really be used on. We fear other countries and cultures, so we commit ourselves to the most brutal politicians, generals, and war merchants, never mind that atomic disaster remains far more likely because of this misplaced trust. We fear the loss of our homes and possessions, so we commit our productive lives to corporations that live pitilessly by the logic of profit, never mind that we deny our own "genius," as Adorno put it, in order to live in what we perceive as the "safety" of "conventional bourgeois standards."

And yet always hovering before us, neglected but still wearing its bright wings, is Wallace Stevens's "necessary angel," the imagination. To socialize the imagination in the way we have socialized fear would be to take up not only creativity but also compassion. There is no such thing as a fascist, a repressive, or even a dominating imagination. That's a contradiction in terms. A fascist imagination could only be an imagination that seeks the death of imagination. Repression is the social imagination committing suicide. In our culture at present, as the Middle Mind illustrates, we commit this form of social suicide on a daily basis. Denying the necessary angel is a chore as regular as taking out the garbage for us. "Darling, did you remember to repress your sense of your own creative capacity before you came to bed? And don't forget to stultify the kids." The imagination's only true concept is freedom—the freedom for humans to create their own world. The mutual recognition that this is what we should all be free to do requires compassion for what others need in their turn. A socialized imagination requires justice.

This is the imagination's sublime. To pursue this sublime will require a revolution of the imagination. I do not know if such a thing is likely, in our world, but I do know that it is possible. Change is real. If capitalism has done humankind no other service, it has shown that change is real. Capitalism knows better than anyone that it must change in order to survive—and it has, brilliantly if maliciously, and all without ever losing sight of its fundamental logic: profit and privilege. We need to learn from capitalism. It would be best if an independent social imagination learned to think change on its own, proactively, because if we must wait for the complete failure of the political violence, militarism, and corporate logic that presently rule our lives, that will be a very difficult and dangerous moment in which finally to try to incorporate the imagination socially.

As I said in my Introduction, we are free to say what we like in today's repressive cultural climate, as long as what we say doesn't matter. Perhaps all I mean by the idea of incorporating the work of the imagination into the social, once again, is that we need to try to say something so that it *matters*. This is no simple undertaking in a political state that is both diffuse and highly controlled. We will know we have succeeded in saying something that matters when we are told that it won't be tolerated. That's when the ruling order of things will show its true colors, as it has in the past (from John Adams's "anti-sedition act," to McCarthyism's pursuit of "un-American activities," to Kent State's emphatic no to anti-war protest, and to the draconian implications for "conspiracy" in the new Bush Department of Homeland Security). When we have succeeded in reviving the social imagination, we will know it by the reaction of those who have most to fear from it.

There is some hope for this revival. Environmental activists like Rainforest Action Network, along with anti-globalization organizers, have made alliances with provocateurs of the imagination like Radiohead, Dave Eggers's *MacSweeney* projects, *Ad-busters* magazine, and political cartoonists like Tom Tomorrow ("This Modern World") and David Rees (*Get Your War On*). These activists and artists, together making "principled play," are attempting to create an alternative social imagination. They will fail in the short run, but they will, I hope, experience the imagination's state of grace in the process. They will feel very much alive. The answer to Stevens's question in this chapter's epigraph—"What wine does one drink" when facing the sublime?—is, as he knew very well, simply this: the feeling of being alive where others are dead is the imagination's only and best wine.

There is no reason for soldiers of the imagination to feel sorry for themselves in the face of certain defeat. As journalist I. F. Stone once wrote,

> The only kinds of fights worth fighting are those you are going to lose, because somebody has to fight them and lose and lose and lose until someday, somebody who believes as you do wins. In order for somebody to win an important, major fight

100 years hence, a lot of other people have got to be willing—
for the sheer fun and joy of it—to go right ahead and fight,
knowing you're going to lose. You mustn't feel like a martyr.
You've got to enjoy it.

And so, we should continue to do what the pragmatists would rec-
ommend: fashion tools to facilitate the revival of the social imagination. Poetry is a tool that does its work, as William Carlos Williams
wrote, in a "hell of repression lit by flashes of inspiration." This book,
too, has been an attempt to fashion a tool. *The Mechanical Bride* is a
tool. Adorno, Derrida, Radiohead, Trow, and Wallace Stevens have all
provided us with tools. We need to learn to use them. If we can learn
to use them, perhaps we will someday answer Williams's question,
"What would have happened in a world . . . lit by the imagination?"

BIBLIOGRAPHY

Earlier versions of sections of this book appeared in *Context, Harper's, Washington Post Book World,* and the *Raleigh Observer.*

All books quoted within this work are listed by author below and named in the text. Each quote is followed by a number within parentheses; this number indicates the page number from which the quote was taken. Citations within the text are from:

Theodor Adorno, *Aesthetic Theory,* University of Minnesota Press, Minneapolis, 1997.

——, *Metaphysics: Concept and Problems,* Stanford University Press, Stanford, CA, 2001.

Harold Bloom, *How to Read and Why,* Scribner, New York, 2000.

——, *The Western Canon,* Riverhead Books, 1995.

Helen Caldicott, *The New Nuclear Danger: George W. Bush's Military-Industrial Complex,* New Press, New York, 2002.

Julia Cameron, *The Artist's Way: A Spiritual Path to Higher Creativity,* Tarcher/Putnam, New York, 1992.

Noam Chomsky, *9-11,* Seven Stories Press, New York, 2001.

Bob Davis, *Speed Is Life: Street Smart Lessons from the Front Lines of Business,* Currency Books/Doubleday, New York, 2001.

Jacques Derrida, *Acts of Literature,* ed. Derek Attridge, Routledge, New York, 1992.

——, *Acts of Religion,* Routledge, New York, 2002.

Dinesh D'Souza, *What's So Great About America,* Regnery, Washington, D.C., 2002.

Richard Florida, *The Rise of the Creative Class, and How It's Transforming Work, Leisure, Community and Everyday Life*, Basic Books, New York, 2002.

Thomas Friedman, *The Lexus and the Olive Tree: Understanding Globalization*, Farrar Straus Giroux, New York, 1999.

Paul Goodman, *Growing Up Absurd*, Vintage, New York, 1960.

John Guillory, *Cultural Capital*, University of Chicago Press, Chicago, 1993.

Michael Hardt and Antonio Negri, *Empire*, Harvard University Press, Cambridge, MA, 2001.

Georg Wilhelm Friedrich Hegel, *Lectures on the Philosophy of Religion*, ed. Peter C. Hodgson, University of California Press, Berkeley, 1988.

Mike Heppner, *The Egg Code*, Knopf, New York, 2002.

Chalmers Johnson, *Blowback: The Costs and Consequences of American Empire*, Owl Books, New York, 2000.

Immanuel Kant, *Critique of Judgment*, trans. Werner S. Pluhar, Hackett, Indianapolis, 1987.

Frank Kermode, *The Sense of an Ending: Studies in the Theory of Fiction*, Oxford University Press, Oxford, UK, 1966.

Libby Lumpkin, *Deep Design: Nine Little Art Histories*, Art Issues Press, Los Angeles, 1999.

Jean-François Lyotard, *The Postmodern Condition: A Report on Knowledge*, University of Minnesota Press, Minneapolis, 1984.

Dwight Macdonald, "A Theory of Mass Culture," in *Culture and Mass Culture*, ed. Davison, Meyersohn, and Shils, Chadwyck-Healey/Somerset House, Teaneck, NJ, 1978.

Marshall McLuhan, *The Mechanical Bride: Folklore of Industrial Man*, Vanguard Press, New York, 1951.

Louis Menand, *The Metaphysical Club: A Story of Ideas in America*, Farrar Straus Giroux, New York, 2001.

Dinty W. Moore, *The Accidental Buddhist*, Main Street Books, New York, 1999.

Dr. Ed Murphy, *The Handbook for Spiritual Warfare*, Thomas Nelson Publishers, Nashville, 1996.

Constance Penley, "Feminism, Psychoanalysis, and the Study of Popular Culture," in *Cultural Studies*, Routledge, New York, 1992.

Ezra Pound, "Hugh Selwyn Mauberley," *Selected Poems of Ezra Pound*, New Directions, New York, 1957.

Joe Queenan, *Balsamic Dreams*, Henry Holt, New York, 2001.

Richard Rosecrance, *The Rise of the Virtual State: Wealth and Power in the Coming Century*, Basic Books, New York, 1999.

Andrew Ross, *Strange Weather: Culture, Science and Technology in the Age of Limits*, Verso, London and New York, 1991.

Theodore Roszak, *The Making of a Counter Culture: Reflections on the Technocratic Society and Its Youthful Opposition*, Doubleday, Garden City, NY, 1969.

Arundhati Roy, *War Talk*, South End Press, Cambridge, MA, 2003 (forthcoming).

John Seabrook, *Nobrow: The Culture of Marketing, the Marketing of Culture*, Vintage, New York, 2001.

Viktor Shklovsky, *Theory of Prose*, Dalkey Archive Press, Chicago/Normal, 1992.

——, *The Third Factory*, Dalkey Archive Press, trans. Richard Sheldon, Chicago/Normal, 2002.

Gilbert Sorrentino, *Something Said*, Dalkey Archive Press, Chicago/Normal, 2001.

Sandra Steingraber, *Having Faith: An Ecologist's Journey to Motherhood*, Perseus, Cambridge, MA, 2001.

Wallace Stevens, *The Collected Poems of Wallace Stevens*, Knopf, New York, 1972.

——, *The Necessary Angel: Essays on Reality and the Imagination*, Vintage, New York, 1951.

George W. S. Trow, *My Pilgrim's Progress*, Pantheon, New York, 1999.

Paul Virilio/Sylvere Lotringer, *Pure War*, Semiotexte(e), New York, 1983.

Cornel West, "The New Cultural Politics of Difference," in *The Cultural Studies Reader*, ed. Simon During, Routledge, New York/London, 1993.

William Carlos Williams, *Imaginations*, New Directions Press, New York, 1970.

ACKNOWLEDGMENTS

Special thanks to my editor, Gideon Weil, for all his intelligence, enthusiasm, and good faith, and to his capable assistant, Anne Connolly, for her useful feminist discriminations. Thanks also to Martin Riker and Chad Post for careful reading and many suggestions for this book, and to Lane Crothers, Chris Breu, and Anne Balsamo, who were kind enough to look at particular chapters. Special special above-and-beyond-type thanks to Georganne Rundblad for years of making most things possible.

ABOUT THE AUTHOR

Curtis White is the author of several distinguished novels, including *Memories of My Father Watching TV* and *Requiem*. A widely acclaimed essayist, his work has appeared in *Context* and *Harper's*. He is an English professor at Illinois State University and the current president of the Center for Book Culture/Dalkey Archive Press.